Building Blocks for Creating a New Life...A Transformational Journey

Linda King-Gulledge & Mabel B. Canada

ISBN: 061563897X
ISBN-13: 9780615638973

Printed in the United States of America

DEDICATION

This book is dedicated to our entire family. Thank you for all your support and encouragement. Know that this book is a labor of love with hopes and desires for all of you to be free to experience life as you would have it. Know that you have within you a gift that longs to be unwrapped, and within that gift is *you*, waiting to create and experience the joys that can be yours in this life.

~With much love! Mabel and Linda

Special Thanks to both, Shireen Canada, Bob Goodson who edited our book tirelessly to help us achieve this dream.

PREFACE

Please accept this gift of love and use it to help you reach your life's desires. Use it to propel through the world of illusion and on to what is truth. Please allow us to help you realize your life in flight, and create the experiences that will bring you to yourself, to our Universal God, the source of unconditional love, and creation...Allow us to share and spread unconditional love to each and every being looking for answers. Know that your questions will be answered, and that the knowledge you seek, should you choose, will allow you to soar. Make a choice, choose, and choose again, until your life is as you would have it. "All you need do is figure out what to do with this life that has been given you."

"How do I know what my greater good is?" you may ask. How are you to know what is best for you, and how are you to know whether or not what you desire is what our Universal God would have for you? These are all good questions, and to put your mind at ease there is one simple answer to them all. If what you desire brings you more happiness, more joy, more love, more peace, and causes no harm to you or another person, than that experience is one that will help you reach your greater good. It doesn't matter whether you desire material wealth, or abundant health, these may be yours. It isn't up to anyone to determine whether or not you are deserving of these things because our Universal God knows you are deserving of everything the universe has to offer. Know that whatever it is your mind can conceive, the Universe can retrieve it, and manifest that desire in your life. Our Universal God says, "Ask and you shall receive." There are no conditions placed upon your asking, just that you ask. As you make a request, learn how to make it with intent by utilizing creative visualization and other skills which will be presented in this book. Learn to move forward without fear of not receiving what you desire. Learn to be confident in your knowledge and relationship with God. Reading "Building Blocks for Creating a New Life" can help you learn that these ideas are not a "get what you want scheme", they are laws of the Universe. Just like the law governing gravity which applies to everyone, and offers the same results to everyone. It is just unfortunate that so many of us have forgotten these laws or have never been made aware of how to apply them.

So many feel lost and disconnected because they are led by their ego which is only self serving and by their deep belief in this world full of illusions. Many have literally forgotten who they really are. There is however beauty in this, the beauty is that many are now requesting from our Universal God source the opportunity to remember again and that is why we offer the knowledge in this book. There are many seeking to regain what has been forgotten, and are seeking purpose; to understand the meaning of this life. After reading this book you may realize that some of the ideas and beliefs you have of yourself and this world may not serve you well any longer. You may learn that you are awakening from a dream state, a life of illusion, and may desire to create a new experience. You may have resigned from the fact that living and existing for the material world is not good enough for you any longer. It may become apparent to you that there is a much deeper meaning to life, and you may begin to recognize the stirring in your soul that may guide you away from this world of illusion and towards the one with a deeper and greater purpose.

Know that you are not alone in this quest for direction and knowledge, you will never be alone. We are beginning to recognize one another and feel the connection between us. We have collectively decided that we are no longer happy just existing in this illusion, we want to know ourselves and one another as who we really are.

Through these thoughts and feelings we have created a means to reach many gifted, loving, awakened, and expressive Beings that have chosen to be part of the divine light which illuminates the world. These individuals have chosen to share their love and knowledge, and to shine brightly like a beacon in the dark in order to help others find their way back home, to our universal God, to our true selves. This book is just one of many means available to help us get to know ourselves as who we really are, and to understand how to make this life work for us in order to experience all things that bring us joy. Building Blocks for Creating a New Life...A Transformational Journey was written with the intention of providing you with tools to help learn more about who you are now, and who you have the potential of being. We want you to know that you are in control of your own reality, and that you create your life's experiences. We want you to understand how your thoughts, feelings, ideas and beliefs affect what it is that you experience in life. We also want to help you learn how to create your experiences and know that there is nothing in your way, nothing stopping you from soaring, other than your own thoughts and fears. We will present information that will help you release old ideas, and embrace the true nature of yourself, and also recognize yourself as being God-like. You have been made in God's image, and have forgotten so.

This book can act as a road map that guides you back to what you were intended to know and experience in this life. Should you choose love, so shall it be, should you choose peace, so shall it be, should you choose abundance, so shall it be. No matter what you choose, "so shall it be" says our Universal God source. You will also learn about the power of "I AM" which sets you on the path leading to your desires. We invite you to walk the path, take the journey, accept the gifts and experiences you create, embrace the truth of yourself, and make the declaration of "I AM" to begin the process of becoming the Being of Love, the Being of Light that you are.

You can make profound changes in your belief system about yourself, and the world around you. You can have a greater understanding of potential, and of the possibilities available to you.

Building Blocks can help you understand the knowledge as to how to further develop your partnership with our Universal God, and learn how to co-create your life anew. We invite you to allow this transformational journey to saturate within you, and allow it to guide you through the metamorphosis that may change your entire life. This knowledge is a loving gift to you. It is yours, it belongs to you, it is intended for you, and it is up to you to step onto the path of a new life, and proceed on to the rest of your life. Enjoy, we send universal blessings and love to you and our universe.

TABLE OF CONTENTS

Introduction. xi

Our Mission 3

One of the Universal Miracles - Metamorphosis 11

Benefits of Building Blocks for Creating a New Life - A
    Transformational Journey. 15

Prayer – The How and Why of It 23

How to Establish Meaningful Prayer 27

Steak and Lobster 31

Partnership 35

Always Reach for Your Highest Self 37

What is Meditation? 41

Guided Meditation 45

How to Begin Meditation 47

Creative Visualization 51

The Creative Journal. 55

Keeping a Journal 59

Affirmations and How to Use Them 63

Personal Inventory Value Assessment (PIVA) 65

Organizing Your Assessment 77

The Journey. 79

Gratitude 83

Forgiveness 91

Health 101

Letting Go of Fear. 107

Overcoming Loss 119

Achieving Clarity. 127

Oneness with Our Universal God 135

Faith. 143

Attraction. 155

Abundance 165

Feeling Worthy 179

Self-Realization 189

Peace 197

Love 207

Transformation Meditation 215

Conclusion 219

Extra Exercises: New Letter of Introduction 223

Famous Quotes 227

Affirmations. 229

Glossary of Terms 231

Some Universal Laws 235

References. 237

INTRODUCTION

Thank you for joining us on what will be a fantastic and transformational journey. We welcome all of you who have chosen to open the cover of this book. We give thanks to our Universal God source for leading you here, and offer that same thanks to you for your choice to come.

You may have been led here because of a need to search for the truth, or because you have the need to better understand the world you live in. You may desire to make changes in your life or to learn to use your creative abilities to manifest your dreams. You may have been led here out of sheer curiosity. The point is that you're here and that indicates that you are seeking something. You may have expectations of receiving something in return for your time, and we're here to help guide you toward those expectations. If you don't have any expectations at this point, our goal is to help you create some.

We want to help you realize that your life can be and should be filled with expectations, without them you cannot create the dreams you desire. We want to help you understand that having expectations is the key to creating your desires. Without expectations you will flounder, you will continue to wait for someone or something else to fulfill you. It is up to you to gain fulfillment, and to create the life you desire. The way to do that is to have expectations, and if you choose a good life, you should have grand expectations! Our goal is to help you realize that your life is yours, it belongs to you, and it is up to you to decide what it is you choose to experience, and in order to create those experiences you must dream. We have created a safe place for you to express your dreams, and will teach you to use life's building blocks to create your desires.

Over the course of the next several days, weeks, or months, (however long it takes you to complete this transformational journey), you will be guided through the process of understanding your life's goals and desires. You will learn to use the images, feelings and emotions, thoughts, ideas, and beliefs to help create your desires. You will be provided with "building blocks" or tools to help you build and construct your dreams, experiences, and desires. While on this journey you will learn to use the power of prayer and will be guided through meditations that are filled with creative imagery that can generate passion, joy, excitement, and gratitude, all necessary states of mind in the creative process. You will be guided through this step by step process, and introduced to creative visualization where you will learn to hold your dreams and desires in your mind which will boost your creative energy, and ability. Throughout this transformational journey journal exercises will be utilized to enhance creativity and inspire powerful day to day life experiences that will bring you closer to your desires.

You can expect a fun, exciting, and challenging journey. One that will cause you to think deeply, evaluate your perspectives, and open your mind and heart to Universal Knowledge which has been kept hidden from you for centuries. We will tap into this knowledge and help you better understand yourself, and help you learn to embrace who you really are with total unconditional acceptance and love.

Come join us on this exciting journey! Discover the joy in life. Reclaim your natural gifts and abilities, and begin living a life of love, abundance and prosperity. Learn to create your dreams by summonsing your desires from the power of the Universe. Rediscover your true connection with our Universal God source, and experience your life in flight!

Welcome. Let's begin…

Building Blocks for Creating a New Life...

A Transformational Journey

OUR MISSION

Our mission is to provide a base of support for the spiritual, emotional, mental development, growth, and well-being of all people in search of wisdom, knowledge, and self-actualization. By sharing the gifts of Universal Knowledge and establishing the belief that we are all ONE, spiritually connected in this vast universe to all things, great and small. We seek to support and establish a Universal connection with people all over the world.

Within this book you will find resources that will assist you in developing the divine gifts that lie within all of us. These are gifts which we all possess, which will begin to re- awaken within your inner soul the moment you realize who you really are, and the power you possess, and what you are capable of creating. We believe that by providing encouragement, and a road map to help you return to BEING loving, kind, accepting, open, and authentic to yourself and others the principles of faith, abundance, clarity, love, peace, gratitude, worthiness, health, forgiveness, and more will be actualized in your life. With these basic, powerful Universal Principals, you can create your life as you desire without limitation!

Our goal is to help spread these basic principles throughout the world in hopes of ultimately joining together in order to spread a blanket of love over the entire universe which could dispel fear, war, hatred, indifference, lack and limitation, and restore the human race to its natural and divine state of BEING. We hope that everyone who chooses to read this book will remember who they really are, and join us in this undertaking of spreading

love throughout our planet in every way possible in order to create the experiences of happiness, contentment, prosperity and
joy which is the divine right of each one of us. Please join us for
a transformational journey of self discovery.

Life can sometimes be like enrolling into college. You've put
in all your elementary work, gotten through the simple stuff, and
are now ready to move onto the more difficult challenges. Much
like college, you decide on a school, select a major or minor just
in case your first plan doesn't work out. You make a commitment
to show up for class prepared, alert, and attentive, ready to take
notes so you can be ready for the small quizzes, and ultimately
the big test. Sometimes it seems that simple, right? Why can't it
be that simple all the time?

There are some people who go through life not bothering
with school at all, let alone enroll or attend college. They just let
circumstances chart their course for them. But once they realize
that their life has no direction, often they quickly see the results
of their poor planning. It becomes clear that they have not set a
life course; they may end up with unwanted events and experiences. If you are one who has chosen to attend the college of
life unprepared, you may show up for class, but bemoan being
there feeling as though you're being force fed lessons which may
be highly distasteful at the very least. What would you say if you
learned that the choices you made, YOUR CHOICES, not those
of your professor, parents, or friends are what chart the course
of your life? What would it mean if you learned that you actually
have complete control over where your life leads and takes you?
Would you give up, would you pay closer attention to your life's
lessons? Would you form a closer relationship with your parents
hoping for more of that possible missed knowledge? What would
you do, and how would you get your life back on track?

Don't worry, we have a simple solution that requires only two
steps, and really they are your most direct and only option for
success. First, *believe* you can change the course of your life,
and second, simply change your mind about the direction you
are headed in. You already knew this right, and weren't those two
steps just too simple? If it were that easy, why doesn't everyone

know this, and if it's all that simple why do you need to keep reading the book or plan for college for that matter? It really is this simple, the problem is that most don't' *believe* it's that simple. The difficult part isn't necessarily changing your mind about something, its believing that after you do change your mind you have the ability, and power to *believe* that you can create the experience you're choosing. That's what most find difficult. Believing they have the ability to create what they want to experience. Take a moment, and evaluate how you feel about this possibility. Ask yourself the question, do you believe you have the ability to create any experience you choose to have? Your answer might likely be "Well, not every experience I desire, but maybe some". If this statement is close to your answer what you've essentially said is, "No, I don't believe I have the ability to create what it is I desire". Your answer indicates doubt, and doubt creates lack, and lack means NONE which is short for NO! We understand that there are many times that even with the information we have we think and feel exactly the same way. The difference is that we fully understand the power of our choices, and we believe, and have faith that we do have the ability to create our desires. In fact you're proof of just that power; you're reading this book right now. That was one of our desires. It's not by chance that you're reading this book, it truly was one of our desires and the Universal Principals we will be discussing will help us show you how we were able to actualize our desire.

Even after proof, many of you will continue to doubt, and that's fair, so we invite you to continue to read on. The information in this book will help you look past your doubt, and move on towards developing the faith you will need to begin creating your life as you would have it. Changing your life really is as simple as changing your mind, and then believing you can do so. The only hard part is to convince yourself that you can. If you can conceive, visualize, and ultimately construct different images of the experiences you desire, you can change your life. For you can only achieve that which you truly believe. The tools that we offer here can be used as building blocks to begin the journey of creating the life you truly desire.

We realize that what appears to be simple in discussion is not always as easy to achieve in reality, which is why we have compiled a group of very powerful tools that will help you develop the Universal Principals that already exist in our universe. They exist within all of us, we have simply forgotten they're here, and because we've not used them, we don't clearly understand how they can effectively help us build, design or create the life we choose. In fact after you realize what some of the principals are you may find it hard to believe they are designed to affect your behavior at all, which is only part of the truth. These principals are really here to be used as signs, instructions, guides, blue prints or building blocks to assist you along the way. When you use the principals and laws of the Universe to aid you in designing your life, you may find that creating your life can be as simple as making the decision to customize the world around you in order to experience your true desires. Your ideas, which we will also call your choices, are connected to your feelings. In other words your thoughts, ideas, and choices cause you to have certain feelings, and those feelings are called your emotions. Your emotions are one of your most valuable tools. They provide you with very valuable information. They act as guides to help you determine when you're on the right path or on the wrong one. They tell you when you're going in the right direction or the wrong one. Your thoughts generate your emotions, and literally cause you to feel a certain way. Try this, think about something, and then evaluate how that thought makes you feel. Now take another moment and consider how very powerful your thoughts actually are. Your thoughts are powerful enough to cause feelings or emotions within you, and those emotions can cause you to make choices and take action. Take another moment and try to think yourself into feeling happy or sad. What are the thoughts that come to your mind when you feel happy? Obviously you're not thinking sad thoughts but feeling happy, and if you are this might be an indication that something might be a little off with the way you're feeling right now. Basically when you feel happy, you're likely to be thinking happy thoughts and imagining something good, or something that makes you happy. It works both ways, your emotions cause certain thoughts just as your thoughts cause certain feelings, and they work hand in hand. In fact because they work hand in hand, learning to pay close attention to your thoughts is a sure fire way not to be confused about how you feel about what you're thinking. Your thoughts are extremely powerful! But using your thoughts to make you feel a certain way isn't their only function. Understanding how you feel goes beyond thoughts and feelings and moves towards something much more exciting, and extremely powerful. This is shall I say, where the sparks begin to fly. When your thoughts and feelings are combined with your beliefs, they literally can create magic. That combination can ultimately manifest your experiences. Your thoughts, feelings, and beliefs create experiences. These experiences are the things you choose, your choices, and your desires, and they make up many of the parts in your life. Now, take a step back and look over your life. Do you like what you see? Are you happy with what your choices have been? Don't worry, it's okay if the answer is "NO", all you have to do is make different choices. But hold on just a second, if you want to do things differently this time and create different or more desirable experiences, why not get a little help so that you can fully understand what you're doing, and assure yourself of getting it right? Why not work on figuring out why things went the way they did before, and get the information you need to rebuild or reconstruct your life the way you really want it this time? Guess what, you're on the right path, you've already made that choice and created the magic that has led you here. This may be a small and simple example of the impact of your choices but a perfect example of your desire to recreate your life. Allow yourself to feel good about this choice. You owe yourself the joy, because you chose well. We have shown you only a glimpse of what lies ahead. We've explained the very basics of what manifesting is about, and you may now understand how your thoughts, feelings, and ideas cause experiences. We will help you understand further that there is only one person in control of your choices, Y-O-U, and that is how you arrived here!

In order for all of this to really make sense, and in order that you fully understand the implications of what you've just read we recommend that you stop here for a moment, (unless you're so fired up and your soul is singing out because it now remembers, and if it does then by all means move ahead). Take some time to think about what you have read. We understand that it will likely take much more information before you can fully embrace these ideas. It would be perfectly appropriate for you to stop and journal about what you've just read, and what your feelings are about it. Give yourself time to contemplate this information especially if these are new ideas for you. In your journal answer the following questions:

- How do I feel about what I have just read?

- How does this information affect my current beliefs?

- What is missing for me to fully grasp, understand, and embrace these thoughts and ideas?

- How might these ideas affect or help me in changing my life?

We understand, this is powerful information, and may be shocking for some people or difficult to digest. It implies that the way you feel, the way you think, and the way you believe about what you feel and think is the reason your life is what it is right now. This would mean that Y-O-U created the life you are now living. It would imply that some of the things you may not like about your life right now are partly your design. But as we said, don't worry, don't fret, don't become discouraged, and definitely don't panic. It can all change, if you truly *believe* and desire, and we can help you begin that process! Let's journey a little further together now.

We know that you don't always feel in control of your thoughts, feelings, and emotions because they are affected by many different things. In fact none of us could possibly be in control of all of our thoughts especially considering that we have well over 90,000 thoughts in a day. In addition, no one could possibly express all the emotions that come from all those 90,000 thoughts. If we were able to react and express all of the different emotions our thoughts might cause, can you imagine the emotional wreck we would all be? Many of the thoughts we have are subconscious thoughts, ones we pay very little if any attention to at all, in fact these are thoughts we are not even aware of. For the sake of confusion, and an in-depth psychological debate, we're going to focus on and discuss your predominate thoughts, the ones you are able to pay attention to, focus on the most on, and feel the strongest about. These are your conscious thoughts.

Many people spend a lot of time thinking about and feeling about relationships so we're going to use relationships as an example to explain one of the reasons you might feel it to be impossible to control your thoughts. If you're in a relationship, your partner's behaviors or actions could affect or cause you to have different thoughts and feelings. Your children affect you in different ways. The people you work with and interact with on your job and in the community affect the way you think and feel, different circumstances in life in general can create feelings and thoughts that appear to be out of your ability to control. We cannot control the actions of another individual, right? While all of this is true, ultimately we still possess the ability to control each and every **choice we've** made. This fact is true from the choice you've made about the partner you've chosen, to the choice you made about the job you chose to accept. With those choices come consequences and experiences both positive and negative. We want to challenge you by suggesting that all but one of the choices we mentioned, you have had a part in creating based on your thoughts, feelings, ideas, beliefs, and choices whether you were conscious or unconsciously aware of them. Again, this may be surprising, but you have in part created many of the circumstances you are currently experiencing. The one choice that may be more difficult to illustrate or prove is the procreation of life if you have children. It might be impossible, especially in the span of this book to convince you that you may have had some control over the child or children in your life; however, by the end of this book, you may possibly develop a slightly different point of view about that subject as well. Let's go a bit further together...

ONE OF THE UNIVERSAL MIRACLES - METAMORPHOSIS

The universe is filled with miracles, and examples of miracles. Each moment, each hour, each day miracles are being performed right before our eyes. Some we see and acknowledge. Others we let pass as just another condition of life. Every day is a miracle within itself, filled with wondrous events that should be acknowledged with gratitude, for they are performances and we are the audience. Consider the flowers at spring, rushing to burst forth, filling themselves with color, design, texture, fragrance, and brilliance. Each evening they rest preparing themselves for the next day's performance when they rise at the break of dawn, yawning, stretching, blushing, bursting with joy, and then settling into them again in full colorful splendor. Each day they wake, excited to perform for us yet again, hoping to touch and soothe our senses and souls. That is a miracle of joy. Flowers are just one of the infinite miracles presented for us to observe. We are blessed with much different life changing miracles, all intended for our joy, inspiration, entertainment, pleasure, and learning. We often go through life taking our Universe's miracles for granted. We are sometimes blind and deaf to its wonder, and often ignore the love it offers, and the intended joy it brings. When we fail to recognize and acknowledge these wonderful gifts it is apparent that we have become complacent to all the gifts that surround us. This complacency can desensitize us to these wonders, and magic of the Universe. Sometimes it causes us to miss opportunities to experience the lovely performances we are gifted with each and every day. There are also miracles that occur in the lives of people across the globe, and throughout our Universe. We hear about countless miracles of recovery, and survival. Though often amazed, we frequently shrug them off after only contemplating their magnificence for a few moments before deciding that it must be some quirk of nature or perhaps a once in a lifetime event. We go on about our daily routines, never giving much thought to the idea that individually, and collectively we have access to such miracles to inspire us, to rejuvenate us, to reignite not only our senses but our deep feelings of passion and inspiration. These feelings of passion can be one of our most powerful tools for creation. What if our daily miracles are intended to remind us, and enable us to do what we've come here to do which is to create our individual and unique experiences! Rarely do we consider that these miracles might be our Universe's way of sending countless signs of not only the magnificence within it but of the miracles and magic that is literally alive within each and every one of us.

It seems that we would sooner acknowledge the strife, sadness, and upheaval in our world, yet pay little attention to its wonders and gifts. We recognize and understand that during this time of upheaval and discontent across the globe, many people are seeking answers to life's purpose, asking why this or that is occurring, and they are desperately seeking to understand how these events fit into the grand scheme of their lives. Our world is also full of distortions, illusions, and as we look for answers it is easy to get lost in the illusion that life is only about material wealth, personal comfort, and fame. These things are not wrong, or bad, they simply are not all there is in life. There is more, much, much more, and our desire is to help remind you of what that is, and to help you find that deeper understanding. It is also our desire to help you remember how to utilize the natural and basic Universal Principals that are intended for all to understand, embrace, and utilize in order to create all the things good in life you choose to experience, no matter what they are.

The information in this book can be used as a tool to help you learn to raise your conscious awareness and understanding so that you can begin to not only feel the connection with the Universe, but also begin to experience that connection with the world around you. Increasing your conscious awareness will enable you to realize and recognize life in a different way. It can help you begin to consciously create the desires you choose with excitement, passion, and love of life. When you view life as a journey full of endless opportunities, and possibilities and love yourself more, and those in the world around you, you can experience the bliss that can only be felt when you are consciously aware of your connection with our Universal God source. Let's move further into this journey together.

BENEFITS OF
BUILDING BLOCKS
FOR CREATING
A NEW LIFE

A TRANSFORMATIONAL JOURNEY

Even the most unpleasant journeys offer some sort of benefit, if you look hard enough. We don't mean to imply that this experience might be unpleasant by any means; in fact it could be the best journey you've ever taken thus far. There are usually trials and tribulations, fears you must face, but ultimately there is an anticipation of joy. There's also usually a certain amount of sacrifice, and compromise necessary but at the end of most journeys your perspective and insight has grown in such a way that allows you to look at life a little differently. This journey in particular offers benefits that are immeasurable. The greatest benefit of this journey is that it can be taken at any point in life no matter where you are in your life, and no matter what your current or past beliefs or experiences have been. It only requires a minimal amount of curiosity about what the purpose of your life might be or a small amount of curiosity about what life is in general. Whether you are experiencing difficulties, unsettling changes, disruptions or bliss, you will benefit from this journey.

Imagine that these new and anticipated experiences posses the ability to set you free from the mundane experiences of a day to day, moment to moment existence. Now, imagine that in order to have these great experiences there is something you must do first. "Ah yes," you may be thinking, "a trick." No tricks, only miracles. Let's refer to this something as a "transformation project." Let's imagine that this "project" might cause you to feel a bit alone at first, maybe slightly isolated from some of the ideas you currently have and have been comfortable with for a while. This "project" may also cause you to feel a bit separate from your current perspective of the world. Remember, this experience won't cause a permanent separation, and that we're only asking you to "imagine." If you were asked to participate for a few weeks, or a month, could you do it?

> * At this time we ask that you take a short break and contemplate this idea. As you do, please record your thoughts, feelings, ideas, and answers to the following questions in your journal. (A free printable journal has been provided for you at www. buildingblocksforanewlife.com

If you were given the possibility of living a life with more purpose, more meaning, more joy, and love, would you be able to let go of some of your current thoughts, ideas and beliefs about the world around you?

- Would it be worth changing your current perspective of life to one that offers a deeper knowledge of yourself and the world you live in?

- Think about how important it might be for you to have the opportunity to change your life for whatever reasons you choose. If you could transform yourself and everything or anything in your life what would you be willing to sacrifice?

- How difficult would it be for you to make these changes?

- If you knew the outcome would be of great benefit to you, what frame of mind would you approach this project with? Why?

This "transformation project" we are asking you to contemplate is similar to the journey a caterpillar must take in anticipation of the true purpose of its life, and the joyful experiences it knows is yet to come.

(A metamorphosis is a change of physical form, structure, conduct or substance by natural, supernatural or unexplainable means.)

Have you ever given much thought to the process of trans-formation a caterpillar actually goes through? Lets' take a short journey together and consider the life of a caterpillar. At first glance the life of a caterpillar may seem mundane, ordinary, perhaps even boring, as it slinks along, up and down trees, over leaves, and often falling prey to other animals looking for a fat succulent meal. However, to the caterpillar, its life is a good life, filled with purpose and anticipation. It appears to move with-out a care in the world. Its movements are slow yet not guarded, sure yet not cautious. It doesn't appear to be preoccupied with its predators, and rarely might you witness it in the midst of its peril. Caterpillars although fragile appear to move about with purpose and intention. Its choices appear deliberate, and it looks as though it knows what it's doing. In fact I would chance to say that the caterpillar's life appears to resemble what life might look like if it were lived with certainty and anticipation. Like a life being lived without a care in the world. The caterpillar appears to live its life anticipating the coming of the "experience" of the transformation, and when it goes through this "experience" of transformation which is also called a metamorphosis; its life becomes actualized. It is when the caterpillar finally experiences its life as whom or what it really is. It might possibly be that this is when we witness its life in full bloom and splendor. When we look at the butterfly it has become, we see it filled with joy because it then knows itself for who it really is, transformed into a magnifi-cent and beautiful butterfly. Although, this journey we invite you to take with us will not really cause you to experience any type of separation, isolation or change in form, obviously, it does sup-port and enable changes within you that could ultimately enable you to feel as though you've experienced a metamorphosis. For some, leaving their old life may remind them of a metamorphic experience or cause feelings of having been shut off in a cocoon, and then awakening to a new and different experience as if being created a new, as beautiful as a butterfly. Some of you may be wondering what a metamorphosis is and how it relates to chang-ing one's life. The definition of a metamorphosis is a change that takes place in form, shape, structure, or substance. It is a means of transformation, as in myths or magic. It could be representative of or create a marked or complete change of character, appearance, conduct, usually a change that takes place after an embryonic state. An embryonic state that we believe many lie within until they rediscover who they really are. The goal is to help individuals awaken from this embryonic state and begin to create experiences of a life taking flight, soaring like that of a beautiful, graceful, and magical butterfly.

We have made our way through the basic understanding of where some people may have been in their lives, and are ready to begin gearing up for this greatly anticipated journey. Let's pack our bags and literally prepare for the journey ahead.

Preparation for a Transformation

Let's look back on and consider the idea of being in at the embryonic stage in life, one that may not necessarily be negative but one that feels without much or real purpose. Perhaps things were going fairly well but you seek a deeper understanding of the world or you have unanswered questions about what happens next.

During the next couple of weeks or so, you will be introduced to powerful tools that can be used as building blocks to begin creating the life you choose. The building blocks will include prayers, guided meditations, creative visualization experiences, creative journal exercises which you have already begun, and the positive and creative benefits of daily affirmations. You will be guided through visualizations and conscious thought that can lead to creating new experiences. This journey can help you through the transformation from that embryonic state of being through the full transformation of a full grown, beautiful butterfly with wings of wisdom to experience your life in flight.

The collection of prayers, accompanied by meditations, and affirmations has been carefully selected, and arranged to address topics in your life which may currently interfere with your ability to establish the connection with the Universe and nurture your creative power. This combination has been selected to help you move past any interferences with purpose and intent. The topics allow you to begin to first identify and recognize who you really are, and what your true relationship is with the Universal God source. The topics allow you to not only reconnect with that eternal source, but also establish a lifelong partnership that will dispel fear and sadness, address loneliness, and depression. These exercises are the key which unlocks the chains that keep your heart, soul, and mind bound and unable to naturally create the desires you choose. The exercises will help you reconnect with your soul where all the knowledge and wisdom is stored about who you really are. You may not be aware of the fact that you already have what you need in order to soar in life; you have simply forgotten how to access this knowledge, and how to reclaim it, or may have never been made aware of it.

You will be introduced to prayer topics which were selected to address several different aspects in life that we all aspire to attain more of. The topics are Love, Peace, Abundance, Clarity, Gratitude, Being Worthy, Oneness, Loss, Health, Forgiveness, Faith, Attraction, Letting Go of Fear, and Abundance. After each prayer topic is a journal exercise that will allow you to establish a deeper connection by learning to manifest these things in your own life. You will then be given an opportunity to practice the skills of manifestation by using the guided meditations, creative journaling, and positive affirmations. You will practice creating new experiences with each topic, and will then journal about those experiences. The guided meditations will help you reach a deeper connection with these topics by also learning to use creative visualization. As you work at your own pace on each topic you will build skills of learning to hold images in your mind for longer periods of time all the while creating strong emotions and feelings that work to bring forth the experiences of manifesting each topic in your life.

You will learn to utilize these skills on different levels and in different capacities teaching you to apply these techniques to your life and other things you may choose to experience. After discovering how to use the building blocks and other tools, you will begin to realize your ability to create the reality you truly choose to experience.

You will learn to recognize the divine knowledge available to you which will help you establish the courage to trust yourself, the Universe, and recognize that you are a divine being entitled to abundance and joy. And you are intended to experience any other aspect of life you choose. Let's journey to develop a deeper understanding.

PRAYER – THE HOW
AND WHY OF IT

What is prayer? Why do people pray? What is the purpose of it? These are just a few of the many questions people have when they are unfamiliar, uncomfortable, or unsure of prayer. Some people wonder not only why we pray, but also question its effectiveness. We believe the reason these questions exist is because many people don't necessarily have a good understanding of what it is, or how it might help them. They only know that it's a ritual that some people resort to in times of need or desperation, and wish for a solution. While many people use prayer, many make these wishes, or requests while experiencing doubt that their wish or request might ever be granted, or are even uncertain if their request is realistic or reasonable. They doubt whether there is a solution, and if there is one, they may doubt whether it's the right one or whether God can or will answer or grant their request. Does this sound familiar to you at all? In the midst of the desperation an individual may be suffering, the halfhearted wish is buried beneath much doubt. *Let's take a break and consider your own feelings about prayer. In your journal answer the following questions.

- What has been your experience with prayer?

- Have you always felt your prayers have been answered? If not why not? If so, why so?

- When you pray have you ever experienced doubt about your prayers being answered?

- If you doubt the possibility of your prayer being answered, what's the real point of prayer?

If you have any doubt about your prayers being answered, it isn't surprising that you may struggle with these questions. Many people are unclear about prayer and may not fully understand how to use it effectively to resolve some of their problems. Let's begin to develop a clearer understanding of prayer.

What is prayer exactly? Prayer is definitely more than just requests and wishes stated or chanted over and over again. Prayer is expressed in many different ways, in music, song, phrases or words. In some societies meditation has been used as a form of praying, and communicating with our Universal God source. The overall belief is that prayer is performed in some type of formalized or structured fashion. The truth is that prayer can be performed in any way shape or form that you are comfortable with as long as it allows you to feel connected with that God source. There is no specific way that prayer travels more rapidly to that source; your intentions are picked up through any means you present it. We believe it's the connection that's most important.

The struggle to understand prayer continues with questions of its effectiveness. Some wonder not only why we pray, but also whether prayer is effective. If there is little belief in anything it is less likely to be successful. Most everyone has experienced or witnessed how ineffectual an act is when there is no belief behind it. We can confidently say that if prayer in any form is saturated in doubt, the individual offering the prayer already possess the belief that their request will not likely be manifested or created. When there is doubt individuals have a tendency to feel that they have to ask over and over again, and sometimes plead. Sometimes the level of desperation is so great that they feel as though begging for permission from God to allow their prayer would be more effective. In addition to all the pleading, and often groveling, many do or feel they have to wait for the approval or for the answer from God before He will "bestow" these things upon them. We believe this type of thinking is incorrect, and almost definitely ineffectual. This mindset limits your ability to create and receive what you are asking for, or trying to experience mainly because there is so much doubt, and also because the belief necessary to establish the connection is not there.

Try to imagine what your feelings would be if you believed it was necessary to participate in a prayer in this fashion. If when you prayed you felt you had to beg or felt you were not likely to receive that prayer, what would you true feelings and thoughts be of the experience of prayer? Would your faith in the results of prayer be great or might it be a bit weak? If you felt this was the only way to communicate your needs, wants, and desires, would you look forward to each and every opportunity you had to pray? Many would not, and as a result of these types of feelings are reluctant to the idea and belief in the power of prayer. Many have been conditioned to believe that this is their only means of expression and so they resign to the ritual and their faith weakens to mere chance.

Let's move together now past these feelings of doubt and on to feelings that offer hope, understanding, and even anticipation in the act of prayer. Because prayer is one of the forms of communication with our Universal God source that we have chosen to use in this book, it is important that you fully understand what it is, how it is used, and why you pray. It is also important to understand just how powerful and effective prayer can be. We hope that as you experience the power in the prayers we've prepared, you will also develop a broader understanding of it, and hopefully you will learn to release the idea that there is a particular ritualistic approach to it in order for prayer to be effective. We'd like to also help you move beyond the thought that there are certain behaviors, sayings, or a particular order which is appropriate for prayer and others which are not. We hope to help you establish an approach that works for you, and the relationship you choose to have with our Universal God source no matter how you choose to initiate it. We hope that you will learn and recognize that there are many different ways to connect and communicate with the Universe, and that there are many different approaches to expression and prayer is but one of those means. It truly is up to you to decide what feels most natural for you or allows you to establish, and feel the greatest connection which will enable you to establish the greatest faith to achieve the results you desire. Most of all we hope to help you believe in your prayers, wishes, desires, and requests, and that they will be made manifest in your life and can come to creation. All that's necessary for you to learn how to pray effectively is for you to shift your ideas, beliefs, and feelings about prayer, and your relationship with the Universe and our Universal God source to one of unconditional acceptance, away from one of doubt or lack.

HOW TO ESTABLISH
MEANINGFUL PRAYER

We've established what individual prayer is for; now let's evaluate a bit more about how to establish your prayer. If your approach to prayer is that you already know your prayers will be made manifest or created in your life, and that our Universe is attentively listening each time you choose to commune, then your approach to beginning prayer will be different. Your confidence and faith can be such that you realize that there is no need to rush into it. You will want to be clear about your intentions, thoughts, feelings, and ideas. Establishing this might be why people associate prayer with sitting quietly with closed eyes. What you will need to do in order to be clear in your intentions, thoughts, feelings, and ideas, is to concentrate, focus, and do that in whatever way works best for you. Many people begin by first acknowledging their gratitude or thanks for what you know will be coming, for what you have already received, and for what you anticipate in your future. It would be important to begin each prayer with this expression of gratitude. It works as a statement of confirmation, belief, and faith. Your expression and acknowledgement of gratitude will be different than anyone and everyone else because your individual experiences are unique to everyone else. Begin by expressing these things in your life that fill you with gratitude. It could begin with an acknowledgement that you have gratitude for being present here on earth this day, or with gratitude for that which has been provided to you. This acknowledgement is your expression of Thanks. You might then begin to pray for your "wishes" or requests and desires, and then release these prayers to our Universal God source. It is important to acknowledge your release because you are stating that you are no longer concerned about "whether", "when" or "if" your desires will be granted. It is your act of faith that says, "I no longer need to hold onto this because I know and believe it will be made manifest or created in my life". You have no concern as to when it will be revealed to you because you **know** our Universal God source has already accepted your request. You are also acknowledging that your anxiety, fear, and doubt have been placed outside of your mind and consciousness, and what remain is your faith, anticipation, excitement, and expectation.

This is a much different frame of mind for the individual praying than most have had. It removes the individual from the submissive role and places them in the initiation, and creation mode. It elevates the individual above hoping, and places them on the level of anticipation, and expectation. This suggests the idea of certainty which is exactly where one needs to be when their faith is without question. Establishing the idea of releasing the prayer may be very difficult for some people because again, many have been conditioned to believe that there is something more they need do in order to make sure God has heard their request, and that He knows how important this request is to them. These are nothing more than thoughts, and behaviors of misplaced doubt. Remember that doubt destroys prayers because if you don't believe it, you cannot conceive it! It's as simple as that! You cannot pretend that you believe either, the Universe knows what's in your mind and heart. Also remember the power of your thoughts and feelings; they are what will assist in the creation of your desires. The sooner you recognize this, the sooner you will be able to release the prayer, and allow the Universe to begin its work manifesting your creation.

Once you have released your prayer, this is a time to quietly go within, listen to the little voice within your heart, mind, or soul. Many times you will be given an immediate answer or indication of your connection, request, and acknowledgement, but because you are not taking time to pay attention, and allow the quiet time after the prayer you may miss this important information. This information acts as your confirmation. It allows you to move forward feeling, and knowing that your prayer is on its way. It allows you to finish feeling excited, and anticipating. Don't worry, if you miss this confirmation or you don't feel it or receive it, the Universe doesn't miss, your message will continue to be received. Be certain of it. Also be aware that these messages can come to you in many different forms. You may hear the message you need in the words of a song playing on the radio, in a commercial on television, in the statement of a friend or neighbor. The message may come quietly or it may come blearing as loud as a fog horn. The point is that if you keep your desire focused in your mind, and pay attention to what's going on around you, you won't miss it. Learn to listen intently, deeply, and purposefully. Try not to second guess yourself, if you receive the slightest inclination of your desire, reach for it, recognize it, and then go for it! We'll work on developing this skill further in the meditation exercises. As you learn to listen you will notice that your perceptions become keener and your vision clearer as new ideas and directions emerge while on this journey toward your new life.

Also, in prayer we must learn to communicate not that what we think we do not have, but what we choose to experience, knowing that it is already present and available in the Universe. The idea of prayer is not that you are asking for experiences because you don't believe you have it, rather you are making a request of your Universal God source to bring forth what you know is already here. This requires a shift in your thinking from submission and asking permission, to offering thanks and showing gratitude as if you have already received your request. This is the idea of gratitude. There is a huge difference between asking for something you want or don't believe you have, and making a request to experience what you know is already available. This is a very simplistic example of the type of thinking and frame of mind we will help you develop. It is as if you are aware that your requests are somewhere in the Universe waiting for you to locate them. You need not be concerned with where your requests are being stored, when it has been manifested it will be attracted to you, and you will receive it. When you choose to make your requests, it is as if you are turning a dial on the radio station, choosing to tune into a particular station because that station has the "music" or requests you've chosen with the directions or locations to your requests. It's up to the Universe to select the actual tune or vehicle in which your request will arrive as well as decide when your selected tune will be played. You simple know that you're on the right station waiting in anticipation to pick up your specific tune or request. To know that your request is already present in the Universe displays a commitment and a conviction of faith in your belief. It also implies that you have total confidence in the Universal God's source to bring forth your requests. "Ask and ye shall receive"; said the Lord. Let's journey a little further in this understanding together.

STEAK AND LOBSTER

Take a moment and imagine yourself sitting in a fine restaurant, looking at the menu there. As you do, allow yourself to imagine the smell of the fragrances and feel of the ambiance. Imagine that you are able to hear the hum, buzz, and chatter of the guests throughout the restaurant. Continue to imagine that after you have been seated in this fine restaurant and as you look over the selections on the menu and decide what you choose to eat, imagine what you might feel after making that selection. Imagine that when the waiter arrives at your table to take your order, you request the steak and lobster. When you place your order in any fine restaurant you never anticipate that the reply from the waiter might ever be, "No, you should choose the tuna salad because, I don't think you deserve the steak and lobster today", that's not likely to happen so imagine that you make the request **knowing** that the chef will prepare the dish to your exact specifications. While you wait for your meal to arrive think about your anticipation of the deliciousness of the meal. Think about your calm sense of satisfaction and confidence about how wonderfully it will be prepared and tastes. Feel the excitement you have, and imagine that you can hardly wait for it to arrive. In fact your mouth probably begins to water just thinking about it. It never enters your mind that your request would be refused, especially since it is listed on the menu, and you've heard how wonderful other people's experiences at this restaurant have been. After you place the order you begin to anticipate it, knowing it will come, imagining your satisfaction with the meal.

Think about the state of mind you would be in when you make the request. Think about the certainty of your expectations. If you happen to be in a restaurant where you received wonderful service in the past or one that has been given rave reviews, you don't worry about whether the dish will please you. You already know it will; you don't concern yourself with how long it may take to arrive at your table because you know that when it does arrive you will be pleased. Those same thoughts feelings, ideas, and emotions should be present when making a request from our Universal God source whether it is through prayer or meditation. Once you make your request, it should not ever enter you mind whether you will receive your request or not because you know that your request is within the ability of the Universe to manifest or create it. You should not be concerned with whether you will be pleased with it or not, because it is an experience you are choosing for yourself, and the Universe is already in agreement with it. You needn't worry about when it arrives because you know that whenever it does you will enjoy it because the Universe's timing is always perfect. "Ask and you shall receive". Making your request is as simple as making the request in the restaurant you just imagined, in fact much more reliable because your request is being made of our Universal God source so there is no question about its perfection. There are no conditions for you to meet, no permission you must have prior to receiving your request, you need only know and believe that what you ask for is already yours. You must have faith, unquestioning faith, and release all doubt, fear, or thoughts of unworthiness.

When you pray, create a mental image of you with what you are requesting and see yourself celebrating the granting of your prayer. Your thoughts have creative power, and your feelings equally possess creative power. The next shift in your awareness should be that when you pray you are using your mind, body, and soul to create the experience of something you believe you need, want, don't already have, or want more of. You must shift the idea of need or want to the idea of expectation and anticipation. Believe it is already so. This concept is very different from the way many of you have been taught to pray and to believe. It requires a shift in the way you feel about your relationship with your Universal God source, and in the way you believe about yourself and your abilities. This shift can be made easier if you think of your relationship as a "partnership" with the Universe. "Partnership" implies that you have a vested interest in the relationship, and that there is some type of ownership on your part in the relationship as well. Ownership implies that you have a certain amount of input, control, and influence as to what goes on in this relationship, rather than being the subservient in the relationship.

Okay, we may be moving a bit faster than some of you are comfortable with, let's slow down a bit so that you can establish your equilibrium. Evaluate what you are feeling right now after reading this passage. Repeat the words or phrases that make you feel uncomfortable because of disbelief, fear, and lack of understanding, whatever. Ask yourself; is it possible for me to have more than a relationship with our Universal God source? Could it be that I actually have some control or even a great deal of control over what occurs in my own life? What does that imply? What does that mean in terms of the responsibility I need to take for my current life's conditions? If this frightens you or makes you feel so uncomfortable that you're questioning whether or not you should continue on then it's important that you consider whether you even want the responsibility it takes to acknowledge that in order to achieve the things you desire you have to think for yourself. You will have to allow yourself to feel things that might frighten you, and to believe things you may not have believed before. The fact is that you have been given the ability to choose, to make choices about your life. This means that there is a certain amount of equality in your relationship with our Universal God source. This might make it a bit easier for you if you understand that being in "partnership" means that the Universe has some say in what occurs in your life, just as you do. It means that you get to make decisions and choices, and ask for assistance in bringing those decisions and choices to fruition. The "partnership" can consist of an equal partnership; in your mind , it could be a 70/30 split or a 60/40 split.

Whichever or whatever symbol of representation you are comfortable with, but it is a partnership all the same. In this partnership you are assisting in the navigation of your life. Your thoughts, ideas, and feelings help chart the course your life is on now and in the future. The desires and experiences you choose to have in your life are being constructed in this partnership. You are not simply subjected to the Universe's desires for you. This is the Universal Law of connection. This doesn't mean that you can only use your ability to choose the situations that are right and wrong or good and bad, but also in choosing what it is that you desire to experience. This power belongs to you as well, and you are co navigating, and creating the life you would choose to experience.

PARTNERSHIP

When you consider yourself in partnership with the Universe you acknowledge that you are assisting in the creation of your experiences. These experiences are being created by the Universal God source through you based on your choices, requests, ideas, beliefs, and feelings. When you consciously take part in your life by actually selecting the experiences that help you reach your greater good, you are taking part in the outcome of your life. You are creating your own reality or self-actualizing. This is the way for life to have true purpose, and meaning. Your direct involvement in what you experience allows you to find importance in what it is that you do. You are not only taking part in creating the circumstances in your life, you are designing the experience, which allows you to claim responsibility, and accountability of your life as well. We understand how frightening this could be if things aren't going so well but imagine the liberation and empowerment you would feel when things are going well, and that's what you're striving for right? This type of thinking is called conscious thinking and feeling and empowers you, and requires that you become more aware of your thoughts, become more selective in the thoughts you do allow. It further empowers you when you are requesting an experience. It encourages you to consciously make choices about what you would have in your life. These choices can and are communicated through your prayers. Being conscious of your requests also helps you develop a deeper relationship with our Universal God source, one that is based on love, respect, and adoration rather than fear, obligation, or forced obedience because you are working with the Universe to fulfill your desires. When you assist in the navigation of your experiences, prayer becomes enjoyable, meaningful, and not an obligation, it becomes desired, not required, it becomes purposeful, not a ritual. Conscious thought and faith is what you need to create life as you would have it. Conscious thought inspires wise choices, meaningful prayer, belief, and a deep meaningful relationship with our Universe.

ALWAYS REACH FOR
YOUR HIGHEST SELF

It's important to remember that in this partnership with our Universal God, you are always working to reach the greatest you can be. This is important because in reaching to attain your highest self, the experiences you create for yourself will always be those that will help you attain your higher self, the better you, your greater good.

As mentioned before, always begin your prayer with gratitude then consciously decide that you would like to have a particular experience. There's no need to justify it or explain it, it is simply what you choose for yourself. There is no need for guilt, permission or submission. Simply make the request then acknowledge or declare that this experience is already in the Universe waiting for you. Many people will struggle for a time with the idea of being direct, confident, and conscious in their prayer. The temptation to approach prayer with submission may always be present because of past conditioning so to increase the power of your prayers, make the request known to our Universal God source by creating a positive image within your mind of what it is in your desire. See yourself with it; study that image, allow yourself to feel the enjoyment of having it. Hold the thought, feelings, and images in your mind for as long as you can. Create the image and feelings of this experience frequently, (day dream of it), study on it, mediate on it, and allow it to become part of you. There's no need to repeat your request, but definitely repeat your image and feelings of experiencing it over and over again. This is the beginning of your lesson of Creative Visualization which we will study later on. Remember your thoughts and feelings have creative power, use them. While creating these images and feelings, remember to resist the feelings of doubt, worry, and fear of when the experience will arrive or if it will be granted. Allow the Universe to decide where, when and how you will receive your experiences. There is never a question of whether you will receive it, know that you will. Now, allow our Universal God source to assume its role in the partnership by deciding when, how, and where you will receive your desired experience.

It is not necessary for you to ask for your desires over and over again, you have been heard by the Universe the very first time. Many think the more they ask, the more likely they will receive. We believe some have confused the importance of repeating your creative images of the experiences with having to ask multiple times. They think the more they hope for this experience, the more "pity" the Universe will have before the experience is allowed, or maybe they think God might forget their requests so they feel they have to remind Him/Her. Hope is a wonderful attribute, but in this case, faith is far more powerful and effective. The more faith you have, the more likely the experience. What affects how and when you receive the experience is your degree of faith, and the strength of your belief, and desire. Let's take a look together at what's behind your beliefs, and desires.

Every living entity on the planet creates and generates energy. This energy is not only physical but spiritual energy as well. Everyone's' energy level is different, and this energy creates and causes a vibration within and around all of us. Some individuals who are naturally high in physical energy may not necessarily have a high spiritual vibration, and vice versa. A person with low physical energy may have a very high spiritual vibration. Your spiritual vibration is effected by your many gifts of insight, awareness, connectedness, psychic ability, creative power, and many other esoteric attributes. Every individual's spiritual vibration level differs based on these many different elements. However, we can consciously affect or increase our vibration level as well. It is believed that the deeper your spiritual awareness, and spiritual consciousness, the higher your vibration. The higher your vibration, the more in line with our Universal power you are. There are ways to increase your spiritual vibration such as increased spiritual consciousness, insightful prayer, meditation can increase your vibration, creative visualization, a heightened state of well-being, good health, having a healthy positive outlook on life, and a high level and understanding of Universal knowledge all impact and can increase an individual's vibration level. Of course our vibration levels fluctuate in strength based on the things going on in our lives, and the things going on in our environment, and our overall mental, emotional, and spiritual health. It is important we create a healthy balance between our mental, emotional, and spiritual well-being in order to establish, and maintain a higher vibration level if we desire a strong connection with the Universe. The higher your vibration level, the stronger the connection to the Universe, the stronger the connection, the more powerful and accurate our communication with the Universe will be. Our images, feelings, and beliefs increase or decrease our vibration. This is why creating positive, pleasurable images that allow us to feel good is important when praying and creating experiences we desire. In other words, the greater your feelings are about receiving the experiences you desire, the higher your vibration or attraction level, which brings you more closely aligned with the experience you are creating. This is the Law of Attraction at work. If you cannot see yourself with that which you choose, you will see yourself without it.

So, learning to believe in your prayers is not only a good thing, it's an essential ingredient in manifesting or creating them in your life. Begin to shift your thoughts about prayer by thinking of the partnership you have with our Universal Good source. Think about what this partnership means to you, how a partnership may change your current relationship with our Universe God source, and how much more empowered a partnership would allow you to be. Allow yourself to accept this idea of "partnership". Remember, you may establish any type of partnership you desire. It's your relationship, and it is always welcomed, and immediately embraced by the Universe. Let's journey to the next phase together.

WHAT IS
MEDITATION?

Meditation is another means of establishing a communication and connection with the powers in the Universe. It enables us the ability to commune with your inner being, higher self, deeper consciousness, and/or with our Universal God source. There are many people who would say that all of these are one in the same, You/God/the Universe. You may not share this belief, and it isn't necessary that you do in order to develop the skills, and experience the benefits of meditation. Meditation allows us to tap into our inner consciousness where we can then access our greater, purer, and deeper reality.

Like prayer, there are many different forms and methods of meditations. Some people are able to reach a meditated state only through concentrated focus, and only under certain conditions or in certain environments such as church or temples. Others use Yoga as a form of meditation, music, art, dance, and prayer can be different methods to achieve a state of meditation as well. Some individuals find that practicing meditation in a room with candles is helpful for them to reach the state of consciousness they desire while others can establish that state by taking a walk in a park of just being close to nature. Meditation is a state of mind and there are many vehicles that can be use to assist you in arriving at that state of mind. It truly can be an individual experience. What might allow you to learn to meditate may not work for someone else. Please feel free to experiment and find out what method works best for you, again, this is totally your individual experience and intended to be enjoyable, not a chore.

In this section of the journey you will learn to filter out, or turn down the "noises" activated by your senses, such as sight, sound, touch, and smell as well as learn how to rid your mind of all the other mental images, and baggage you may carry around with you. Our busy world is filled with external stimuli, and information. It is often difficult for our brain to process all that is going on around us. Many people report experiencing headaches, sometimes constantly because their brain simply becomes overloaded, or over stimulated from all the clutter, noise and thinking that it does every waking hour. It isn't surprising that we crave for opportunities to escape. The appropriate and healthy way to escape from it all can be found in meditation. These discomforts can become very overwhelming. Many people find it difficult to function in our world and use other means to filter out the noise. Some of these methods may even be self-destructive. In order to maintain inner peace, and establish the ability to maintain appropriate direction, people often choose to meditate. They may meditate simply to rejuvenate themselves; others find meditation an important and beneficial factor necessary before making decisions or conducting daily life. One of the main benefits received immediately from meditation is the attainment of clarity and the development of the ability to listen deeply. Sometimes gaining clarity allows you to detach from the surface of reality and connect with the deeper inner core of your consciousness making it easier to understand and tolerate the external world and all that is in it. Many report that when this happens they feel as though they have been taken to a heightened level of spiritual awareness.

If you have never meditated before, think about the idea of being able to sit quietly and not have any thoughts enter your mind. Yes, that's right, while meditating it is possible to not think about anything, not what to fix for dinner, not what to shop for at the grocery story. Pure and simple, "quiet" can be very refreshing, and empowering. Many people are able to clear their minds to such a degree that their mind appears to be totally blank for a period of time. Reaching this state of meditation can also be very difficult, maintaining it can seem impossible for some. After you have learned to control your mind and are able to let go of the "bouncing" thoughts, which is usually exactly what happens when you meditate. In the beginning you may experience thoughts traveling very quickly in your mind, or they may linger making it difficult not to concentrate on them. This is all a normal process when learning to control the activity of your mind, it takes practice. The more you practice, the better you become at it. It may seem difficult to let go of what teachers of meditation for eons have called the "monkey mind" which is the mind that jumps from one thought to another. This condition is usually very typical, but with practice can be mastered. There are many different techniques in meditation some difficult to obtain but for the sake of this journey we will utilize guided meditation to accomplish our goals. For most this is one of the simplest forms of establishing meditation. Learning through guided meditation is the ground work for deeper meditation study.

GUIDED MEDITATION

We have designed guided meditations that initially do not require total detachment as do some deeper meditations techniques. Rather, you become involved and interact in the meditation as you are projected and guided using words to create images, and scenes into a deeper state, and are asked to mentally engage your mind to create specific images and experiences. As humans we already engage our minds in this way so it will be much easier for you to engage in guided meditations here. We strongly suggest that you read the guided meditations through before you begin them. Some readers might find it helpful to not only read them through first but may choose to record them as they read them out loud. This creates a truly guided meditation, and allows you to be less active during the exercise freeing you to focus on only establishing the connection and reaching a deeper state of meditation. Recording the meditations will allow you to lead yourself, step by step, without the need to break and read. The other option would be to have a meditation partner where your partner reads the meditation for you and you read it for them. Mediating with a partner can be very beneficial and uplifting as you share your experiences and provide encouragement for one another. Should you decide to record your meditation you can be as creative as you like as long as you do not change the essential content of the meditation exercise.

You may want to select quiet music to play softly in the background as you recite the meditations softly or you may ask someone you know with a pleasant and soothing voice to record them for you. It is completely up to you, and for your total enjoyment.

HOW TO BEGIN MEDITATION

Here is a quick guide to meditation for beginners, if you are already experiences with meditation you may find these steps very simplistic and easy to achieve. To begin:

1. Block out a certain amount of uninterrupted time anywhere from 15 minutes to 30 minutes to start with, longer if you choose to have a deeper experience of if you feel the need to move slower through the process.
2. Find a quiet place as far removed from noises and distractions as possible.
3. Find a darkened room; it seems to be more conducive for meditation or an area that is dimly lit.
4. Get comfortable; loosen anything that may be tightly fitted.
5. Have the intention in your mind that you are going to meditate.
6. Sit comfortably, either on the floor, pillow, or chair, which ever suits you and provides you with the most comfort. You can be in a lying position if you choose.
7. Gather your thoughts; begin to focus your breathing. Position your hands comfortably in your lap or at your sides.
8. Take in and release three deep cleansing breaths each time you begin.

9. Quietly still your body, and listen to the sounds around you, maybe what you hear is the refrigerator or the distant sound of children playing. Whatever you hear, acknowledge the sound, and let it go. Don't try to figure it out or form a mental image of it, just acknowledge that you hear it, and let it go.

10. Read the meditation or have a recording of it to guide you through. You can also incorporate other things to enhance the experience such as soft, relaxing music, candles, incense, or scented flowers; it's completely up to you.

11. When using creative visualization during the guided meditation, find a focal point, it could be a flower in a vase, a light that you envision in the center of your forehead, or just practice the simple act of listening to the way your breath sounds as you breathe in and out, then in again, and out.

12. When you feel as though you don't know your "nose from your toes" you are in meditation. So in other words when you begin to feel weightless, so still that you are unaware of the weight of your own body, you will have reached a state of meditation. Do not be disappointed if you are unable to experience this feeling right away. It may take you a time to establish this level of meditation. With practice you can get there. If it continues to be a struggle for you, determine how you feel when you are moving through the process and make the adjustments you feel you need to.

13. After meditating, allow yourself to return to the present by first wiggling your toes or fingers. Begin to return by opening one eye very slowly, establish your balance, and slowly open the other eye. As you open your eyes you may feel a little lightheaded, so sit quietly for a few more moments to regain yourself.

14. Often during these quiet moments after meditation, ideas and messages may come to you, so always have a pencil and paper at your side to jot down any information you may receive immediately after the mediation or while you were mediating. You may gain more clarity and receive

information about a certain source making it easier to make decisions or understand something that you may have been struggling with. The effects of mediation can linger with some people for hours; others come right out of it. It is a very personal and individual experience. Make sure your allow yourself to enjoy it.

You will find that after meditation you will be noticeably calmer and relaxed. You may react differently to stressful situations and you may begin to develop a deep sense of knowing as though you have been sleeping and are now awakening to a new but familiar world.

Meditation may be a new experience for some of you, and others may feel very comfortable with it and have their own methods of practice already established. For those that are less familiar with meditation, let's take a moment to explain it a bit further. Meditation actually means to ponder on something with intent, usually continuously and deeply or to study long and hard on it to gain deeper sense of awareness of it, and clarity of it. For those of you who are new to this experience you may find it difficult to achieve the full effect the first few times and may struggle a bit to simply hold a thought without being interrupted by another invasive thought. What we can offer for encouragement is to be aware of your mood and select a time to meditate when you are able to be relaxed and at ease. As stated earlier, meditation takes practice, the more you do it, the better you get at it. Plan when it is most appropriate for you to meditate. Do not plan a session if you are in a hurry or are expecting company or on a time line as the idea of being rushed will keep you from totally relaxing and being able to let go. Remember that there is no special body position you need have or no special way you should sit. Just make sure you are comfortable, relaxed, and at ease.

CREATIVE
VISUALIATION

Creative Visualization is a very important and extremely powerful tool which will be used throughout this journey. You will be asked many times to "imagine or to "create an image in your mind" of something. These are forms of creative visualization. You will be asked to use creative visualization during the course of the prayers, meditations, and journal exercises. It has wonderful benefits, and can be used as a tool in learning to manifest experiences that will help you reach your greater self. Let me take a moment to explain what creative visualization is and how it can benefit you. The idea of creative visualization is that when you are able to create a vision of what it is you desire to experience in detail, the information about that image is projected into the Universe as a request and the Universe shifts to duplicate or create that request, allowing it to be made manifest in your reality. If your mind can perceive it, your brain can see it, and then our Universal God source can conceive it, thus create it. When you use creative visualization you begin to unlock the limits of your mind by giving yourself permission to create images that then assist in creating your experiences. It also allows you to tap into the Universal law of attraction that works to move you closer to aligning you to the things you desire to experience. When you focus your attention on a particular subject or event or thing, you are creating the act of "requesting" the Universe to retrieve that desire. Of course there is much more involved in this process such as the law of attraction, and quantum physics, but on this journey we're taking we'll move at a pace that will allow you to grasp things one step at a time. There are many other resources and books available that can present a perspective of these elements, this book is more about what you have control of, and your role in the creation process. Let's move on a little further.

The more detailed your thoughts, and the more passionate your feelings are about your desires, the clearer you are able to visualize them. Your excitement about receiving your desires and experiences is important. The more excitement and anticipation generated, the more powerful your request to the Universe. Excitement and passion generate deep emotions. When your deep emotions and desires are combined with your visual images of those desires, an instant and very powerful connection occurs and becomes a request from you to our Universal God source of your desires. That request is instantly transformed into creative power. That process is how your desires are   manifested into your reality. Of course this is a very simplistic description of what actually occurs but what is most important to know is that when you combine strong emotions with visual images of your desires, magic can literally be created. Understand that just as you are able to attract and create positive experiences in your life, you are able to do the same with negative experiences as well.

Concentrating on a particular thing, situation or event creates an image in your mind. When your thoughts, feelings and desires are filled with fear, anxiety, and worry, you may not have the experience you desire. If fact you may accidentally create a negative experience instead. Sometimes you create an experience and have it manifest immediately while other times it may take much longer to materialize. The duration of time it takes to create an experience, and when it actually arrives depends on many factors, and is left to our Universal God source's knowledge and judgment. What you should remember is that it isn't a matter of whether you might receive it, it's a matter of whether you believe it, and that all paths are clear in your mind in order for it to arrive. During journey we will focus specifically on how to create the images of your desires, and also how to hold those images in order to establish clarity, focus, excitement, and passion for what you choose to experience.

During the creative visualization exercises we will present you with different tasks that will help define the desires you choose to experience. You will practice creating images or visualizations you might have for a particular desire or experience, and also practice developing conscious thought to further deeper your awareness of the possibilities of your creations. Please understand, creative visualization is not unique only to those reading this book and taking this journey. It is the same for everyone. We all use this tool to create many of our desires; many are simply unaware of its power, or use, and/or practice utilizing it unconsciously. This journey simply helps you recognize and consciously achieve the desires and experiences you choose.

*Feel free to use the journal of your choice but upon purchasing this book you have been provided with a free printable journal. You can retrieve it for free from our site at www.building-blocksforanewlife.com

THE CREATIVE
JOURNAL

As part of your journey we ask you to keep a creative journal and record the many different experiences that occur during this process. A creative journal is a journal that utilizes specific information to help prompt you to create your very own visions and ideas. Keeping a journal will allow you the opportunity to learn from your experiences. The prayers, meditations, affirmations, and journal exercises used on this journey will also help you establish the clarity to re-create the images you desire to experience. The visions and ideas you have will be unique to you, and although everyone taking this journey will be working from the same prompts, each will create their own personal and specific visions. Once you begin performing the different exercises, you will be asked to record the experiences and daily activities you have. The creative journal is intended to be used throughout this journey, and beyond should you choose. It is intended to act as your companion. For every experience that occurs while on this journey there will be specific information you will be asked to record. The journal will offer a place for you to record not only your experiences but also your thoughts and feelings.

Using a journal may be the first for many of you while some of you may be very familiar with the joys and benefits of journal keeping. You will find that not only is journal keeping beneficial while on this journey but will also be beneficial after completing the journey as well. Journal keeping can be very powerful because having a place to record your thoughts, and ideas on an ongoing basis can help relieve stress, keep you focused and on task, help provide a means of reflection and encouragement. It can help you become more organized, and assist with maintaining order in your everyday life. Keeping a journal provides you with a place to release worries, doubts, and fears, and work out the questions you may have in your life. It also allows you to address issues you struggle with in a safe, private and healthy way. We strongly encourage you to continue keeping your journal because although this book will end, your journey will continue, and what you experience will be worth writing about!

Learning to understand yourself, your beliefs, thoughts, feelings, strengths, and areas needing improvement is very important to your personal and spiritual growth, and development. Having this knowledge can help you better understand why you think and feel a particular way. Understanding yourself can also help you determine what affects you, what inspires you, what motivates you, and it helps you determine what you need to become a better you. Developing this knowledge of "self" can provide countless benefits to you, and can help chart a path that will lead you closer to where you want to be in life. It inspires and creates conscious thought and knowledge of who you are. This journey has designed exercises that will help you develop this knowledge of "self".

We will present you with an opportunity to take inventory of your personal thoughts, ideas, feelings, beliefs, fears, and desires. You will be able to evaluate this information and use it to make the life changes you feel necessary to create your desires. This exercise will be included as part of your journal keeping exercises.

The responsibility of keeping a journal may be difficult for some, and may come very easy to others. Many people find it comforting to write about changes and events that take place in their lives. Some of you may find it a chore to write a letter to a loved one let alone keep a journal. Keep in mind that the written word has proven to be very powerful. It allows you to connect with a part of yourself that lies closer to your true emotions.

Don't be afraid to unleash your true feelings, you may be surprised at what you learn!

When prompted to journal, allow yourself to think on it as an enjoyable exercise. Learn from your experiences, and learn to value the experiences enough to want to record them for future reference. The importance of keeping a journal is more than just the idea of recording events and information; it is a form of self-expression. For this purpose we use and suggest that you pay close attention to recording the life changes you experience as it will be a great joy to revisit this journal experience over again after you have completed this journey. Also, as you go through this life change, this transformation (metamorphosis), you will gain knowledge and insight that will aid you as your life takes flight. Each exercise from the prayers, meditations, and affirmations will produce experiences and change; some may be so profound that you will want to remember and recall them. It will be important that you have an accurate account of these experiences, journaling them will help you achieve that. When journaling remember to take your time and enjoy the process.

KEEPING A JOURNAL

You will have many different experiences and reactions as you move through this journey. You may receive information that you can apply to your life directly or indirectly. You will absorb and apply some of the information right away, and may have to ponder, evaluate or assimilate other information. You will need to have a means of evaluating the information and experiences you have. It will be easier for you to access this information if it is located in one place, is accurately organized, and recorded. Like prayer, and meditation, journal keeping is a personal and individual experience. There are no specific techniques or style that is required. Some people are very artistic and use illustrations and drawings to record their experiences. Some may choose to write volumes, others prefer to keep short notes. It truly is up to you, however, the things that will help you with organization will be to always enter the day, date, and time of each entry as well as the topic which you are journaling about. Some people journal daily, some twice a day, morning and night. Again, it is your choice but we recommend that you journal every time you are working to complete an exercise.

It is important that you are open and honest when your journal. Try not to filter your experiences and try not to be too vague in your descriptions and narrations. In fact, allow yourself to accept whatever it is that you receive as a gift from your inner self. Make a choice to be as descriptive as possible, you will be happy, and appreciate that you did when you revisit the journal at a later date. Remember a very important part of this journey is to learn to create images of what you experience, and of the desires you choose to experience. The more you use your journal, the more comfortable you will become with recording your experiences. Also remember that there is no right way or wrong way to make entries, just information that will help you know yourself better, and information that will aid you in charting your course more accurately.

Journals are your private thoughts, feelings, and ideas. However, some thinking of keeping a journal much like blogging, and do so with others. You may choose to share some of the information with a close friend or family member. You may even have a journal buddy, where the two of you or group of you share with one another what you have experienced or what may be going on in your life. You are encouraged to keep your journal in whatever way is most comfortable to you. As you begin to embrace the exercises, and apply the lessons, you will find that you will not be limited to receiving information only during times you are reading or completing an exercise. You may receive information throughout the course of your daily life. Many people allow themselves to journal several times through the day. You may choose to journal at a specific time but if you choose a specific time, be prepared to jot down notes as you receive information or are led to different experiences. Developing consistency is also important when establishing a journal, especially as you begin this life changing journey.

It will be important for you to be able to evaluate the different changes that occur in your life while on this journey. You will want a record of where your life was when you began this journey, and you will also want a record of what changes will take place along the way. This is the most accurate way for you to determine the actual changes you have made. It will be important for some of you to reflect back to where you were, and how far you were able to advance. You will have notes of what works for you, and what does not. Upon your completion of this journey, you will be amazed at how different your ideas and beliefs may have changes. You may learn something about yourself that unlocks years of emotional grief, and releases you from baggage that has weighted you down for years. These revelations alone could be life changing. It is very likely that you will want to have the process recorded.

Expect to have wonderful things take place while you are on this journey, and allow yourself to experience all of the excitement, and anticipation that looking back on your progress will bring. Get ready for an exciting time, expect it, anticipate it, love, embrace, and enjoy it.

A brief note about selecting your journal

When you select a journal for this journey or for any reason, select one that inspires you. Think about the things that inspire you most in life. Think about the things that make you feel good or bring you comfort. Ask yourself what it would take to inspire you to keep a journal, and want to write in it? Are you an individual that is motivated or inspired by pictures of nature, animals, and pictures of the ocean or of Paris? Are you an individual who is inspired by the feel of a particular kind of writing instrument gliding across textured paper? Are you inspired by the feel of a leather bound journal or are you inspired and most comfortable writing on a small ruled college notebook? These considerations are important because the more you now about what inspires you, the more likely you will be to follow through with using it. Once you have made the selection, decide what type writing instrument you will use. Some people can't write with a pencil comfortable, and prefer a pen. Decide this and have whatever you will use near your journal. Make your journal experience as comfortable as possible, enjoyable, and convenient as possible.

Try to make it a point to write the day, date, time if possible, the exercise you are journaling about, and any affirmations you may have selected that appeal to you.

Beginning Your Entries

When recording your journal entries we suggest the following format, ultimately it is completely up to you.

1. Make a journal entry for each exercise, prayer topic, and meditation.
2. Select an affirmation from the list of affirmations provided or select one of your own.
3. Move on to the creative journal exercise, and make sure you journal your entire experiences even if they carry over onto another day.
4. You may feel led to make an entry at other times, please feel free to journal freely.

You will notice a quote or affirmation at the beginning of each prayer topic which will apply directly to the prayer and/or exercise itself. The quotes or affirmations are uplifting, insightful, and may add meaning and purpose to some of the exercises. Feel free to record them in a special section of your journal if you are struck by one or all of them.

AFFIRMATIONS AND HOW TO USE THEM

Have you ever given any thought of the power in a word? Consider the power in a group of words. Affirmations are such groupings of words. They are among the many tools available to use that help us grow, develop, and move towards the connection power in the Universe. Affirmations are a group of words that create a phrase or sentence(s) which strike enough power to provide encouragement, support, motivation, inspiration, and move us toward action. They can be very powerful, and often influence our thoughts and feelings in a completely positive way. An affirmation can be a quote or statement someone has made that sheds great knowledge and provides great inspiration. It usually projects positive images, thoughts or feelings, and may touch an individual in such a way that lifts the inner being or soul. An affirmation can also cause an elevation in an individual's spiritual vibration. They are sometimes so powerful that they remind us to hold ourselves in an elevated and positive state of awareness and feeling which helps to generate creative power.

We have chosen to use affirmations for this journey because many of them possess the ability to help sustain and elevate vibration levels as well as a heightened state of awareness. We want to provide you with tools that will not only help elevate your thoughts, but help remind you of what it is you are aspiring towards. Along with each prayer topic you will find a choice of three affirmations. You may be led to select a particular affirmation which you should use throughout the exercise to help encourage, support, motivate, and inspire you in the life changing experience you desire to experience. You can also alternate between the affirmations, use them as you are inspired to do so, or you can select your own. After you have made a selection from the three choices, record it into your journal. We also invite you to write them on sticky notes or pieces of paper to carry along with you or put in places you frequently look such as on the kitchen cabinets, the refrigerator, bathroom mirror, your computer screen, calendar, or post it anywhere you would likely see the affirmation and be reminded to shift your thoughts to a more positive state. We encourage you to use the affirmations in whatever way you are led, the important thing is to use them, read them, say them out loud, write them, think them, share them, and seek to **Be** them. Remember, they are powerful, beneficial, and valuable tools for you to use in order to help you become more successful in getting where it is you want to be.

There are many, many statements, and quotes that can be used as an affirmation. One very important, and powerful affirmation that was shared with us by a very dear friend, and one we would hope for you to remember is:

"The power of the Universe moves with every
thought you think!"
~Susie Sheldon

PERSONAL INVENTORY VALUE ASSESSMENT

The Personal Inventory Value Assessment (PIVA) is a tool used to access your thoughts, feelings, ideas, and beliefs which help you determine whether you are able to create the vibration necessary to achieve your desires. This tool can be used to help you learn more about your personal and individual belief system. Processing this information allows you to evaluate your beliefs and target, and identify specific areas they you may choose to change. It will also help you determine the emotional content of your beliefs. Having this information at your fingertips makes it easier to pinpoint those issues that may interfere with your ability to reach your greater self in order to create your desires. Completing this assessment is an essential step in the process of this journey. The assessment will also help you determine the effect these beliefs, thoughts, and ideas currently have on your life.

While on this journey you will begin to recognize how different experiences cause you to think, act, feel, and believe. It is important to know what may have shifted within you or your life, or may have changed altogether. As these changes occur, your life circumstances will be affected, and may change as well. It will be imperative to your success to have this information. Before you begin it is important to evaluate what your current beliefs are. Finding out who you are now, what your values are, what your beliefs are, how you feel about particular things prior to this journey will help you determine just how much your life was impacted by those past experiences. This tool will aid you in evaluating your transformation (metamorphosis), and help you understand the differences between your new thoughts, feelings, and beliefs, and the old ones you may have chosen to change. We will begin by investigating your belief and value system. To better help you understand the full impact of this life changing experience; we will ask you to retake this assessment and record your findings at the completion of this journey as well.

The tool we have chosen to help gather this information throughout this journey is called a Personal Inventory Value Assessment or PIVA. Your assessment will be unique to you and your thoughts and beliefs. It is specific to you and your life, It will depict some of your thoughts, core beliefs, and values, but it is not who you really are, it is simply part of what you think, feel, and believe. The good thing about the PIVA is that it is not set in stone; it can change as easily as you can change your mind or beliefs.

When you are affected by an experience, it brings you insight and impacts you in certain ways that causes and form your beliefs. Those thoughts and beliefs form and shape your values as well. You can look at this assessment as an opportunity to create yourself anew, to be who it is you truly want to be. This is special information about you, created by you, just for you.

Investing the time to take a close look at yourself now, will allow you to learn exactly what you need to learn in order to make the changes or shifts in your life that could help send your life soaring. Along with this list, there will also be a series of questions that will help you further gain perspective, information, and knowledge about who you believe yourself to be or who, by the end of this journey you really are.

Let's take a short journey and look at what values are, and how they affect what we believe, and how those beliefs cause us to conduct ourselves. Values are concepts that shape our thoughts, they help determine the worth or value of our experiences, and the different things in our lives. Values help guide how we act and feel about things and experiences. They are not measured in terms of "good" or "bad", and they can change and fluctuate as well. Our values affect every part of our lives, from the choices we make, to how we determine where to live; we are all greatly influenced by our values. Some of our values we may be consciously aware of, and the others we are not aware of them at all, they are subconscious. Many of the values we have were learned at such an early age that we have become conditioned into accepting how they make us behave or feel. They're affects cause us to have "automatic" behaviors and feelings. We are often completely unaware of how they cause us to behave and act. Once these values are brought to the surface, we become aware of exactly how they affect us. We can then do something to change or shift our thoughts and behaviors to accommodate our choices, rather than have these them cause reactions. When we think about our values we become aware of them, conscious of them, and can then respond to them with more thought and intent. A response is considered a thoughtful act, one we are aware of and have given specific intent to. Looking at your values is how you will begin to evaluate your personal inventory, PIVA.

There is one very important point to make and be aware of regarding values. An individual's values are not a means to judge character. I realize that many people use this type of information to sum up who they think a person is. We are using this tool to help you gather information about yourself, information that you may have been aware of but most important, information that you are unaware of and choose to change. Remember, there are no good or bad answers, just answers that will help you determine the thoughts, feelings, and beliefs you might like to change. What follows is the assessment that you will take now, and will also be given the opportunity to take it again, if you choose, at the end of this journey. Please record this information in your journal for further evaluation and discussion.

Listed below are some values that affect all of our lives. We're going to use a rating system to determine preferences. You will be asked to use a scale of 1-3 to indicate how important these values are to you.

> Please refer to your journal to record your responses to the following information. Your free printable journal can be found at <u>www.building-blocksforanewlife.com</u>

(Rate each as a **1** which indicates "not at all", **2** indicates "somewhat important", **3** indicates "extremely important").

Determine how important these things are to you:

- **Personal satisfaction:** "I want to feel worthwhile" _____

- **Relationship:** "I want to improve the relationships in my life: _____

- **Self Esteem:** "What people think and feel about me is as important as what I think of myself" _____

- **Self-Respect:** "I like and respect myself" _____

- **Self-Worth:** "I value and respect who I am" _____

- **Power:** "It is important for people to look up to me" _____

- **People:** "I enjoy the company of others most of the time, and enjoy spending time with others" _____

- **Money:** "I don't feel I am earning my worth, having more money would complete my happiness" _____

- **Enjoyment:** "I have things in my life that I enjoy" _____

- **Environment:** "I have a clean and healthy environment which supports my spiritual /emotional growth" _____

- **Job Security:** "I am employed doing what I love, and feel I am secure and compensated fairly" _____

- **Spiritual Development:** "I have a solid base in my spiritual life, and I have the help I need to support it" _____

- **Personal Growth:** "I am happy with who I am and my accomplishments" _____

- **Independence:** "I enjoy being alone and don't needs others to feel fulfilled" _____

*(If there are other values that are important to you that are not listed, please add them to your list)

Value Inventory

List the top **(10) ten value** words, from 1 to 10. in order of their importance to your life:

____ balance	____ environment	____ change
____ excitement	____ loyalty	____ abundance
____ responsibility	____ recognition	____ accountability
____ cooperation	____ accomplishment	____ friendship
____ family	____ power/control	____ flexibility
____ respect	____ hard working	____ companionship
____ diversity	____ honesty	____ community
____ health	____ competition	____ charity
____ security	____ respectability	____ spiritual development

____ communication	____ variety
____ helping others	____ challenge
____ structure	____ personal growth
____ education	____ fairness
____ independence	____ discipline
____ prosperity	____ opportunity

From your value inventory list, indicate your top **five (5)** values that are of the most importance to you at this time:

We have reached a point in the book where we ask that you begin recording responses in your journal. Please refer to your journal and record the necessary entries at this time

Record Your Journal Responses to the Following Questions

Why are these things important to you? (Give explanations of all five choices)

How is their importance demonstrated in your life?

What are your two most important accomplishments that involve these values?

How are these two accomplishments important to you, what do they represent?

What three things do you like most about yourself?

What things would you like to change about yourself?

What is your main motivation for change or improvement?

What is the single most important thing in your life that you would like to change?

Why is it important that you make this change?

How would that change impact your life?

If you were able to **choose**, how would you go about making that change?

What are you able to do about it now?

PERSONAL INVENTORY LIST

(Listed below are traits that may help describe you, record 5 of the ones that apply to you as 1 being extremely close in description and 5 being less descriptive of you:

_____ tenacious	_____ resourceful	_____ tolerant
_____ responsible	_____ imaginative	_____ outgoing
_____ versatile	_____ persistent	_____ decisive
_____ honest	_____ expressive	
_____ helpful	_____ optimistic	
_____ cheerful	_____ organized	
_____ independent	_____ tactful	
_____ loyal	_____ caring	
_____ energetic	_____ negotiable	
_____ flexible	_____ pleasant	
_____ open minded	_____ hopeful	
_____ spontaneous	_____ insightful	
_____ friendly	_____ motivated	
_____ approachable	_____ sociable	
_____ humorous	_____ sensitive	

PIVA RESULTS

L et's take a look at what you may have learned about yourself. Now that your PIVA is complete, and you have the information right in front of you what many people take for granted about themselves, it should be a less daunting task to assess your values, ideas, beliefs, and feelings. With this information you can begin to make more conscious decisions about what it is that you would like to change in your life. It may help you better understand why you have made some of the choices in your life, and also help you understand some of your future choices. You have a working idea of the things that are important to you at this stage in your life, as well as an idea of the specific things that you would like to work towards improving. This outline can be used to guide you towards where you want to be. It can help you decide the attitudes you may want to adjust, and help with knowing what action is necessary to make some of the changes necessary for you to create your life as you would have it. This information enables you to develop a conscious awareness of what you think is important, how you feel about those things and others, and what you believe about yourself. The information you gathered in the PIVA may be new to you, or it may provide you with a better perspective of who you are, which will make it a bit easier for you to begin the work necessary to make the changes you feel are important to you.

After this life changing journey, it is our hope that you will learn even more about who you actually are, and realize that you truly are a very remarkable, unique and special individual. You are an integral part of the power in the Universe, without you the world would not be the same! It is important for you to know that!

At the conclusion of this experience you will have the opportunity to re take this assessment, and compare the information here with what you gather at the end of this journey. You will be able to determine, just how your experiences during the journey may have shifted or changed your thoughts, feelings, ideas, beliefs, and values.

ORGANIZING YOUR ASSESSMENT

A s you recall, this assessment is neither good nor bad. There are no right or wrong answers simply information that allows you to determine whether you are satisfied with what your thoughts, feelings, ideas, beliefs, and values are. Many of you may be very proud of what you believe and feel. Some may realize that after completing the assessment there may be values and beliefs that do not suit who you choose to be, or they may not suit the desires you choose to create.

In your journal begin by simply recording the information you gathered in the PIVA. Remember to begin your entry with the day, date, (time), and list it as **Current PIVA** results, and then complete the following steps:

From the values list, determine the values that you selected as being the ones that are **extremely important** to you, your 4's and 5's.

List the ones you selected as being **somewhat important** to you, your 3's and 2's.

Then list those which you selected as **not at all important** to you (1).

Next, select the first five **(5)** values you selected to define things that are important to you

Select the **(5)** which best describe you.

Study this information. Think deeply about how it might define your current beliefs. Determine whether these thoughts, feelings, and beliefs suit what you would choose as thoughts, feelings, and beliefs of you **being** your highest "self".

In your journal write a narrative describing yourself and your beliefs using your current values. Include your ideas from the selection of questions you answered.

What have you learned about yourself? Are there any values you would choose to change, if so what are they?

Determine why making these changes are important, and how would making these changes affect your life?

Are you satisfied with the information from your PIVA?

Determine what steps you might need to take to make the changes you chose.

THE JOURNEY

All journeys require a certain amount of planning. When one embarks upon a journey there are certain expectations, hopes, desires, and a certain amount of anticipation involved. We have instructed you about the tools that will accompany you on this journey. You have a greater perspective of what they are, how to use them, and how they can be used to benefit you. Based on what you learned from your PIVA, you may now have a better understanding of the things that are important to you. You may also better understand exactly what your values are, and can now begin using this information to create your hopes and desires. The results of your PIVA may have provided you with information that might help you understand what your expectations are as well. Sorting out this information can allow you to feel better equipped to create your experiences specifically, and consciously. This information becomes a key ingredient to building your life the way you really desire it.

You have made a commitment to yourself to explore the possibilities that are available to you in order to create experiences that will allow you to soar in life. When you chose this journey you made a conscious choice to embark upon a journey of change that may bring about a transformation (metamorphosis). Your thoughts and choices created an action, and caused the Universe to shift which began to move in a new direction for you. Your desires motivated you to seek out information that you felt you did not have but wanted to experience. It is our hope that you allow your desires to help you create an experience that will leave you with a new sense of peace, creativity, and direction.

Your bags are packed, and you're ready to go. Let's begin this journey... Here we Go!

Beginning The Journey
Fourteen (14) different prayer topics have been selected. Each prayer topic is accompanied by three different affirmations, a guided meditation, and journal exercise. The topics have been categorized and aligned with the five seasons based on the Chinese calendar. It is our belief that the closer you are aligned with the Universe, the stronger the connection with the Universe.

We have chosen the Chinese calendar because of its documented and historical accuracy. In 2700BC, a Chinese scientist named Da Rao Shi was given the task of creating a calendar. In doing so he became the first to record, calculate, and measure time. He performed the extraordinary feat, especially for the time, of painstaking recording the changes between the sky, earth, and the four seasons. By using these calculations it is believed that this calendar is closely aligned with the patterns and changes in the Universe. His calculations and ability to measure time has enabled this culture to record their 5000 year history in chronological order. We to believe it is the calendar closest in alignment with the Universe. Because we seek to achieve proper alignment in order to establish a strong connection with the power of the Universe, we have aligned each prayer topic and exercise with the season that most supports its efforts. The prayer topics and season of alignment are as follows:

Season: Late Summer - is the season that calls for gratitude and great fullness. The prayers that fall under this season are, **Gratitude, and Health**

Season: Autumn - is the season of acknowledgement and release. The prayers that fall under this season are **Forgiveness, Loss, and Letting Go of Fear**

Season: Winter is the season of stillness, deep listening, and inner strength. The prayers that fall under this season are **Faith, Oneness- Establishing the Power Within, and Peace**

Season: Spring is a call to skillfully strategize. The prayers that are in alignment with this season are **Clarity, Attraction, and Abundance**

Season: Summer is the season that is a call to deep purpose and mission. The following prayers fall under this season **Feeling Worthy, Self-Realization, and Love**

Surely these prayer topics and exercises can and should be practiced as you see fit, and as they fit into your life at the time of your choosing. We have simply added this information to help create a more powerful connection with the Universe. If you should choose to practice the topics in a different order we have no doubt that they will be just as effective. Remember this is an individualized journey; we are only your guides.

GRATITUDE

**"The best and most beautiful things in this world cannot be
seen or even heard, but must be felt with the heart"
~Helen Keller**

This prayer will help you to remember gratitude is an expression of appreciation for that which we have received, as well
as that which we anticipate.

Prayer
Today I choose to celebrate gratitude. Each day I become more
aware of all that I have to be grateful for in my life, and I offer
thanks. There are so many things that I often take for granted;
from the vast and limitless sky full of the most radiant star, to the
depths of the ocean which cools and bathes the earth with its
waters and the rich soil that nourishes all the beautiful trees and
flowers. All these things that I may take for granted, I now honor
with love. When I stop and place my focus and attention on all
that I have to be thankful for I realize that whatever my life circumstances, my heart can be filled with joy and gratitude. I also
realize the love of our Universal God source shines like a beacon
upon me. When I put my attention upon it I recognize it's healing and cleansing power and give thanks for its warmth. This
light enables me to see all the blessings in my life, and brings into
focus the people, experiences, opportunities, love, and joy that is
mine. I now extend gratitude to the breath within my body, the
sight which my eyes behold, the sounds which my ears hear, the

smells which my nostrils capture, the feel of all that I touch, and the knowledge and awareness which I possess within me. I know that when I openly embrace gratitude my life becomes fuller, and I am filled with love and appreciation. I hold in gratitude all experiences and events in my life, and know all is well in my world.

Gratitude Meditation

To begin this meditation, select a quiet and serene place. We will take a journey together where we will assist you in establishing a connection with nature.

As you prepare to relax by taking in a large cleansing breath, slowly release it. Repeat this step three times each time allow yourself to relax a bit more, second deep breath, settle into yourself, third deep breath, let go of all that weights your mind and body. As you establish your comfort and clarity begin to visualize that you are in the middle of a forest surrounded by rows upon rows of tall green trees. Observe how they grow, stretching and reaching for the sky. As you take in this beauty and wonder take notice of how these trees spread their branches stretching outwards seeking to touch one another. Look onto the branches of these trees and follow their branches outward and notice the fruit or flowers they bear. As you think on these trees, imagine all the ways they help affect your life, and the life of the planet. Think about the oxygen they provide us, the shelter they provide so many different animals. Imagine the shade, and coolness their majestic trunks hold. As you imagine their wonder and gifts, allow yourself to feel the gratitude you have for all they are. Hold in your mind the images of these trees, and focus on the feeling of gratitude they allow you to have. Hold on to the feelings of gratitude. As you take notice of the feelings of gratitude, begin thinking about your day and the events you are able to recall which you are grateful for. Take a moment to extend your gratitude for those events whatever they are. Think on your family, and friends, your home, and job, your health and strength. As you imagine the branches reaching, stretching, and seeking to embrace one another, also imagine that you are in the middle of the forest surrounded by the trees as they embrace as if including you in what feels like a gentle hug. Think on your events of the day, and as you do don't judge them; extend those strong feelings of gratitude toward them, and realize that each event has occurred just as it has in order to achieve the experiences you have chosen.

Remember

Although we rarely understand things as they occur in our lives, know that they are happening for a perfect and exact reason. Learn to embrace every event by extending gratitude to the pleasant events as well as those which are unpleasant. Being in the state of gratitude elevates your thoughts and feelings far beyond your normal state of consciousness and awareness, allowing love to flow smoothly and freely through your life, and putting you in line to receive what it is you desire.

Gratitude allows you forgiveness without effort; it allows you acceptance and tolerance of that which you may not understand.

Affirmations/Quotes:

- "I give thanks each day for all of life's wonders and am awed by its beauty".

- "All is well in my world and I extend love and gratitude to all things in it".

- "I accept and expect goodness, and am grateful for all the good currently in my life and for that which I anticipate".

Journal Exercise on Gratitude

**~"Gratitude unlocks the fullness of life. It turns what we have into enough, and more. It turns denial into acceptance; chaos into order, confusion into clarity. It can turn a meal into a feast, a house into a home, a stranger into a friend. Gratitude makes sense of our past, brings peace for today, and creates a vision for tomorrow."
~Melody Beattie**

Today is a wonderful day to practice gratitude, because no matter where you are in life there is so much to be grateful for every moment of every day. Even if your life is not yet what you want it to be, life without gratitude would clearly be less. So let's begin to recognize and acknowledge all that there is in your life you have to be grateful for. Begin by compiling a list, a list of gratitude which will include all the things in your life that you feel has benefited you in one way or another. You are free to include things like the air you breathe, your perfect body functioning in perfect harmony, your creativity, your ability to communicate, or perhaps it's your ability to listen and be helpful to others. Consider all your blessings, and add them to the list.

As you compile this list, work to expand it beyond what is familiar to you. Think deeply, and focus on things that would normally escape your memory. You may wish to show gratitude and appreciation to the mail carrier or perhaps your bank teller, or maybe to your gardener for the work he performs on your grounds. Consider anyone who performs even the smallest of deeds that affects your life in the slightest. As the list grows you can review it often and each time you do, it will help you realize all the true blessings you have in your life.

Many times we take so much for granted but when you take the time to pay attention and to acknowledge the presence of even the tiniest of blessings, you begin to realize that your life is much fuller than you may have previously thought. Displaying gratitude and offering thanks helps to elevate your mind, and when you elevate your state of mind, you elevate your creative energy. When you take the time and put forth the effort to extend gratitude to ALL that you have, you attract even more positive experiences that often arrive in the form of love, joy, peace, and prosperity.

Remember, it is not only important to extend gratitude to the things and people we love, but also to the more unpleasant or undesired things in your life as well, for they help to reinforce gratitude and remind you that no matter how unpleasant the experience, you can always choose again, and that is an awesome reason to be grateful for. Including the unpleasant or undesirable experiences also allows you the opportunity to learn and grow both spiritually and emotionally.

Gratitude List

As you work to create you gratitude list, notice your state of mind. While you work on this exercise you should notice a sense of well-being because it is impossible to be sad or depressed when you are in the state of gratitude. Keep in mind that extending gratitude is like giving a gift to someone else, a gift of thanks. Most people who give a gift rarely feel bad about doing so. Giving is an act of service, and should always be done with a kind and loving heart.

After your list is complete, read it through, select a few entries from the list that you would enjoy writing a brief thank you note to. For example, if on your list you stated that you feel grateful for your courage, the note could read: "I am grateful for my courage. It has allowed me to face many tough situations, it has helped make me feel strong, and trustworthy..." or if you listed that you are grateful for your teller, you note might say, "I want to extend gratitude to my teller. Each time I go to the bank she greets me with a smile and makes me feel important even when I only have a few dollars in my account, she is always accurate when tending to my account, I appreciate her sincerity"... Once you have written the thank you note for the virtue, subject, or person put the notes into a small box or small container, and label it the "Gratitude Box". Each day or as often as you choose, select a few more topics from your list and compose a note for, choose from the list, and compose a note until you have completed the entire list, and place the notes in the box.

The next step is that after each item on your list has received a written thank you, and is placed in the box, while there it is "held in gratitude". Set the box near an area you use to complete your morning routine, and as you prepare for the day, select a note from the gratitude box and read it feeling your gratitude. Hold that item in gratitude, and return it to the box. In the evening, select another note, and keep making a selection until the thank you notes from your gratitude box has been selected and read out loud.

Some of you may choose for this to be an ongoing project, especially if you have created a very long list or of you choose to continue to add notes to the box. What a wonderful way to continue to experience extending and receiving gratitude. What a wonderful and often unexpected gift for someone to receive. You may even choose to take this project a step further by not only writing the thank you not but actually delivering it to the individual you are giving thanks for. While you are involved with this exercise, notice how your sense of well-being increases. In fact, gratitude is so contagious; don't be surprised if you begin receiving unexpected "thank you" notes, gifts, hugs, smiles, or other signs of appreciation and affection. That is what gratitude causes, a giving of thanks, and love that flows through you, into another, and back again in abundance.

In your journal make the following entries, and answer the following questions:

- From your list what were the 10 most important things you felt most grateful for?

- How were you affected emotionally after participating in this exercise?

- Did you have any unexpected experiences while practicing this exercise?

- Had you forgotten to extend gratitude toward someone/thing before participating in this exercise, if so what was it?

- What changes have you made in your life as a result of this exercise?

- What will you do differently to achieve this level of thinking and feeling more often?

- Conclude your journal entry with a statement that extends gratitude for the experience and all that you have learned as a result of this lesson. Also, make a declaration to continue to experience well-being, and sustain it now that you have gained the tools to help create it.

FORGIVENESS

**To forgive is to set a prisoner free and discover
that the prisoner was you.
~ Lewis B. Smedes**

This prayer will assist you in recognizing the aspects of your life where Forgiveness is needed in order to release and heal the pain left behind.

Prayer:
As I travel this circle of life, I come to the realization that when I think I have reached the end, I embark upon a new beginning, and it is through this continuous journey that I experience growth and transformation. I am aware of all that the universe and I have created together. I am aware of all the many wonderful skills and abilities I am learning to develop in order to experience my life as I would have it. I am gaining clarity in my vision, I am experiencing inner peace, and I am beginning to attract the positive experiences that help reinforce my connection with the Universe. I am learning to embrace myself and those around me; I have gained more faith as every day the Universe bares new gifts to continue my growth. I am in a place where I can see all that I have to be grateful for. As I learn to embrace myself unconditionally, I also feel strong enough to face and let go of some of my fears. All these experiences have strengthened my life, and continue to encourage and support my growth and development. My next step is to begin to heal from that which I feel has caused me injury emotionally, physically and

psychologically. Although I perceive these injuries as real, I must learn that they are mere illusions and figments of my imagination as I am one with the power of the Universe, and nothing can truly harm me. In order for me to heal from these injuries, I must learn to forgive the injury itself, as well as the individual or situation that has caused this harm. Just as I am learning to let go of my fears in order to move beyond them, I must also learn to forgive and let go of the feeling of hurt, shame, disappointment, anger, and rejection. I know that I am more than these feelings, and that as long as I hold love within my heart, I am ever protected from any illusions of harm. When I choose love, forgiveness becomes an easy task, and releases all the power these feelings have held over my life. As I choose love, I gain strength and courage to face these hurt feelings and dismiss them as they are insignificant in the presence of that which I am, Universal Love.

Forgiveness Meditation

For this meditation prepare to be undisturbed for at least 30 minutes. Select a place where you can be quiet, peaceful, safe, and undisturbed. As you become comfortable with you environment, begin to think on things that bring about calm, peace and quiet. Begin to quiet your mind, slow down your thoughts and ideas. In order to create the image we will create together, imagine that your mind is blank. Go even deeper, as you do you gain more peace, quiet, and relaxation. Allow your body to become losses and relaxed, and feel yourself at ease. Now, begin to visualize yourself walking along a path in a very peaceful and beautiful park. See the park and its tall green trees, allow yourself to smell the fresh scent of the trees. Also allow yourself to feel the warm breeze blowing across your face, and as you do, take notice of the sounds around you. Begin to focus on the sounds the trees make as they are rustled by the wind. Now imagine that you hear the sound of the birds singing from the trees, and the sound of the scampering of the squirrels and chipmunks. As you walk further into the park you notice a lake where you can see ducks and swans floating effortlessly on the water. You can also hear the squawks from the geese, and ducks. Along this path you now notice the beautiful flowers that are painted in rows of colorful beauty. You notice flowers of all kinds, and of all colors. You come aware of the fragrance of the flowers and take in the sweet smell as you remain on this path. Just ahead, you see a park bench. As you arrive imagine yourself sitting upon the bench continuing to take in all the beautiful sights, sounds, and smells. Allow yourself to remain there in this peaceful and beautiful place for as long as you like, enjoying the refreshing and relaxing feelings that come from this place. As you sit noticing now the sky you are moved to see a light veil of clouds dusting the brilliant blue sky. Slowly lean your head back on the bench and allow it to soak up the warm rays from the sun. As you do you go into a deeper state of relaxation where you now feel fully connected with everything in the park. You are connected to all the joy, the beauty, the relaxation, and the calm that surrounds. Bask in the joy of this place and the entities here as you are one with it all.

You may remain here for as long as you choose but whenever you decide slowly begin to take notice of the shift that has begun here. Notice the wind blowing against your face is now blowing a little harder. Notice that the sound of the trees has changed, and they now sound more like someone is shaking them. Imagine that you also hear the sounds of the animals in the park as they become a bit more still from the pickup of the wind. Imagine that you can also see the birds and ducks on the lake as they begin to swim away, seeking cover. In your mind's eye, see the once brilliant blue sky slowly move to light gray, and then onto a darker gray. It is now obvious that a storm has approached and has caused the wind to blow even stronger. With the wind comes the rain, and it has begun to fall from the sky in sprinkles. You begin to move away from the park bench but before you are able to get far, the storm displays itself in full force. Imagine that you are caught in the midst of this storm, unable to move away. In every direction you turn you are met with now pounding rain, and winds that are now ripping at your hair and skin. As you struggle to see, the rain begins to pound the earth which you can hear, and sounds like the pounding of a small drum. As you continue to imagine what it would feel like to be caught in this storm, fear begins to creep within you. You notice that you are now feeling anxious and worried as the wind and the rain continue to assault you. This assault continues, and as it does you become even more afraid, and worry about how long the storm will last. As you stand caught in the park, you have feelings of helplessness, you also feel powerless to do anything to help yourself, and your must simply stand and weather the storm. Allow yourself these feelings, remain there with these feelings even though you may be very uncomfortable, and give yourself a chance to have the feelings you are experiencing. Once you have taken note of how you feel in the midst of this storm, you can begin to decrease the intensity of the storm by thinking on who you are. Begin to think on your connection with everything in the park. Imagine yourself as one with the trees, and now one with the flowers, and one with all the animals in the park. See yourself as one with everything around you, even one with the storm. Imagine that you send and extend love to all those things you are now one with. As you reach this union and oneness, you notice that the storm is not so intense. The wind is calming down and the rain that once pounded the ground is now moving away and it is now only sprinkling. Allow yourself to feel the decrease in the intensity around you. As the rain moves from sprinkles to nothing at all imagine and feel your feelings of powerlessness dissipate, and you begin to experience a new found feeling of optimism and hopefulness.

Affirmations – Forgiveness

- "I forgive and express love easily and effortlessly."

- "I set my past free by extending forgiveness and love."

- "I easily forgive others, and I am easily forgiven by them."

- "I release my past injuries from my mind, body, soul, and consciousness. I am free."

Journal Exercise – Forgiveness
The purpose of this exercise is to begin to create the spirit of forgiveness within your life. Forgiveness is a process for many people. In certain situations and with certain individuals, forgiveness can be offered immediately. It can be as simple as deciding to let go of a transgression and deciding not to allow it to hold you captive by negative emotions. It can be as simple as that, for some, others may have to work at it.

Forgiveness is a wonderful experience, and can greatly enhance your entire life. We understand that under certain circumstances it can seem very difficult if not impossible to achieve, it may even seem unimaginable. Working to forgive can often evoke such deep emotions and feelings of pain, resentment, anger, and shame that the act can be paralyzing. If you notice, I called it an "act" because that is exactly what you must do. You must take action, and it requires your decision to participate in the actual "act" of forgiving. You must make a decision to forgive and move on or remain in the feelings of being held hostage to those negative and hurtful feelings, memories or ideas. You must also believe that whatever the injury caused can be healed. This belief is very important because if you feel the injury is so damaging that healing is impossible, you will likely struggle with the act of forgiving. You must reach the understanding that there is nothing that love cannot heal. You must understand, no one can hold you hostage and force you to feel guilty for injuries you may have caused them, nor do you have to remain angry and bitter for injuries someone may have caused you. Only you can reclaim your personal power and release you from feelings of guilt, fear, anger, resentment, or shame! You cannot control what others feel or choose to think so you must focus on freeing yourself through love, and forgiveness. You should also work to release others from their feelings of guilt and shame be learning to forgive them.

There are certain incidents that will be more difficult to move beyond but the sooner you do move beyond them, the stronger, and happier you will be. Forgiveness allows you to feel free!

You will need four specific items for this exercise. Please make sure you have these items before beginning. You will need a large piece of paper, pink or red marker, crayons or color pencils, an envelope, and your journal. First begin by logging the entry into your journal, date, day, and journal exercise. On that page begin by selecting and logging your Affirmations. Now begin listing the names or events that have caused you harm. Think about the things you feel you are experiencing difficulty moving past, things that when you focus on them cause you to feel sadness, or pain. As you work to create this list, be careful not to allow yourself to recall the actual experiences in detail, and try hard not to attach your current feelings to those memories that come up. Work at not allowing those memories to rekindle old emotions. Also be careful with the images of those memories you allow in your mind. Remember, your thoughts have creative power. We are not intending to re-traumatize or bring up explicit memories of old wounds; we are working on creating a means to be able to let them go.

After you have completed the list, take a moment to reevaluate the names and events on your list. Begin to imagine the weight of emotions those contents bear. While the page you have written on may appear almost weightless, its contents create a huge weight in your life. As you feel the weight of these names, events, and memories, make a declaration to release this weight from your mind, body, soul, and consciousness, and write it down. Understand that the only place this amount of weight can be held safely is in the heart, full of light and love. In the presence of love everything on your list can become weightless. The feelings they represent can once again become as weightless as the sheet of paper they are written upon.

On a separate sheet of paper, one that can be separated from your journal pages, draw a large heart shape. Use the red or pink crayon or marker to color the inside of your heart. As you color your heart, imagine that the color you have chosen bursts with love. What this drawing represents is you filling your own heart with love. Color the inside of the heart in completely; try to imagine nothing but love inside that and your own heart. Once you have completed filling your heart with love, look at it, feel it, see it filled with love. Now select a name or event from your list and write that name or event inside the heart of love you just created. As you write each name or event call it by name, and say these words:

"... I render you weightless, and release you to this heart of love and light."

With each name, complete this statement, and feel the joy and weight lifting from your mind, body, and soul. By casting those injuries and wounds to love; you are allowing the healing process to begin. You are freeing yourself with LOVE! After you have completed the process of transferring each name, event, and memory to your drawn heart, your heart of love is filled with the injuries and wounds you feel you have or feel you may have caused, imagine embracing each individual or event with love and light. Feel the love you would extend to those injuries. Also allow yourself to feel gratitude for being able to let them go. Imagine how freeing it is to no longer carry the weight they caused you. Imagine yourself rejoicing in this release. See yourself weightless; imagine your feet lifting off the ground. Imagine your heart filled with love, and joy. Imagine that you are now free from all the excess baggage you carried for so long.

Now, as you rejoice, take the heart, filled with love, and fold it so that it fits into the envelope you have. Place it into the envelope and on the front of the envelope write: **FORGIVEN!**

(There will never be a need to reopen this envelope as these injuries have been forgiven. You may discard it as you choose, but the wounds inside are being healed!)

Then recite this prayer:

"I give thanks to our Universal God source for filling my heart with so much love and forgiveness. I have allowed myself to remain trapped in my feelings of sadness, resentment, anger, and shame. Today I make a conscious choice to reclaim my personal power, and offer forgiveness to those who have caused me harm, and I also forgive myself for any harm I have caused oth-

ers. I understand that the only way for me to move beyond this state of mind is to accept and offer love. Love is the only healing power, and its power lives within me. Through love I can let go of my past, separate myself from past injuries and wounds, and look to the future with loving anticipation of all things good and healthy. I extend gratitude to our Universal God source for bringing me this gift that allows me to be healed."

Remember:
Forgiveness can be a process, there are some injuries that may be compounded with other issues that may require more time, work, and love in order for them to be forgiven. No matter the length of time it may take, the only way to heal all wounds is through love so keep extending love to yourself, and others. Work hard to replace all negative emotions with love. The more you work at creating the loving experience of forgiveness, the sooner it will manifest in your life. (Side note, if ever you begin to feel old feelings from the memories, and events sealed in the envelope, pick up the envelope and recite the prayer of forgiveness, and continue to move forward. You can do this, I know you can!

HEALTH

A bodily disease which we look upon as whole and entire within itself, may, after all be but a symptom of some ailment in the spiritual part of ourselves. Look within for healing first.
~Nathaniel Hawthorne

This prayer will help you move through the obstacles that can block your vision and perspective in order to achieve perfect health.

Prayer
Today, I affirm that I am One with the perfection of the Universal God source. I realize and accept that there is only one mind, and one sprit. I look not through the eyes of others, but through eyes of clarity, and knowledge that I am connected to and made in the image of God, which is perfect. As I reflect upon on the awesomeness of this realization, I am aware that every cell of my body is balanced and in rhythm with the Universe. I now proclaim that there is only room for love in my heart, and I dismiss any thoughts that are opposite of love. Love offers a healing power, and I embrace that power within my heart, mind, and soul. Unloving thoughts about me or others manifest in my body as unbalance, pain, blockage, and illness. I surrender to the love of our Universal God source which washes away all doubt, fear, worry, and negative thought. My body is whole and healed. I keep watch over the words I utter and the thoughts I allow to enter my mind. I claim perfect health, for I AM One with the Universe, and the God Source in the Universe is perfect. Therefore, I claim perfect health.

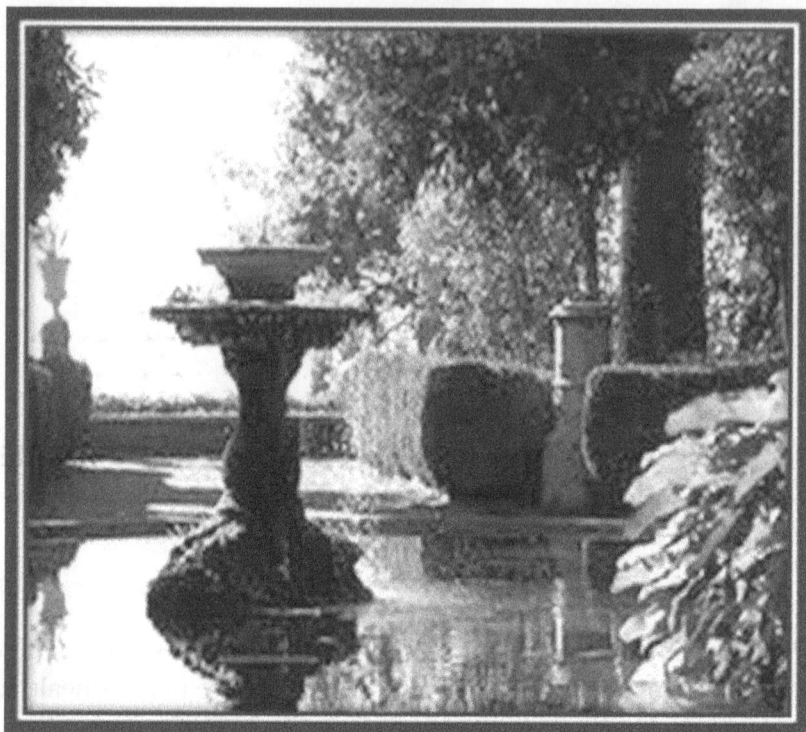

Health Meditation

In this meditation you will begin as with all other meditations we will guide you through. Create a comfortable place for yourself, allow at least 15 to 30 minutes of uninterrupted time. Before you begin, get into a comfortable position, and begin by taking and releasing three deep, cleansing breaths.

Imagine yourself standing at the top of a spiral staircase. The staircase is illuminated in a bright warm light that reveals every step. There is no need to worry or be concerned for your safety as this warm light assures that you will be safe and well protected. Imagine that you begin to take your first step down this stairway. As you begin to move down, you smell a clean refreshing scent in the air. Looking around, you see tall, beautiful urns lining the staircase. The urns are filled with beautiful, blooming flowers. With every step descending the stairs the fragrance of the flowers becomes more and more pleasant. As you continue down and reach the bottom of the stairs, imagine that you see a beautiful marble fountain filled with fresh spring water. Look at the water as it gently cascades down the fountain, falling in silvery streams into the basin of the fountain. After you've reached the bottom of the stairs, imagine yourself stopping to pluck flowers from one of the urns. The vivid colors of the flowers make a beautiful bouquet as you circle the fountain, picking one flower after another. Imagine the sound of the cascading fountain, and feel the warm and pleasant breeze against your skin, and the slight blowing of your hair the force of the water creates. Imagine yourself remaining here enjoying the feelings of freshness, beauty, and wholeness you may feel. At the fountain you find a crystal goblet that you take into your hands. Imagine that you bend down to the fountain and fill the goblet with the silvery streaming water. See yourself bringing the goblet to your lips to drink of the cool sweet fluid. The cool water fills your mouth, and slowly trickles down your throat. As you drink, imagine that you feel the water as it moves through your body, cleansing, and healing every organ in your body. When you have finished drinking, you put the goblet down and find that you are illuminating with the same bright light that led you down the stairs. You ascend the stairs, still carrying the bouquet of flowers as of various colors and scents. The flowers are a gift to you, reflecting the wholeness that you have as you leave with the idea, and feeling of perfect health.

Remember

Illness can be caused by the confusion in your life or the past memories of pain, and fear. If you allow these thoughts to fester in your mind, your ego can take over, and cause you to feel separated for our Universal God source. This perception of separation can cause you to feel ill.

<u>Affirmations for Health</u>

- "Today I claim perfect health".

- "I send my body only loving thoughts which will create the experience of perfect health".

- "I take perfect care of my body, mind, and sprit".

- "Love creates health and well-being, and that is what I choose for my life. I hold thoughts of Love and Good Health."

Journal Exercise on Health

~"the concept of total wellness recognizes that our every thought, word, and behavior affects our greater health and well-being. And we in turn are affected not only emotionally but also physically and spiritually."
~Greg Anderson

Today you will work on developing and increasing your awareness of how to sustain and maintain good health and well-being.

We will learn more every day, how what we think about is reflected in how we are living our lives right now. We are affected not only by our life style, but first, and foremost we are finding that our thoughts and feelings have a direct and often devastating impact upon on our health. Without knowing so, we have the ability to and do actually "think" ourselves into illness. Have you ever said or thought something to the effect of: "I get a headache every time I…" You may have noticed that shortly after making that statement, you begin to have the experience of having a headache. Our thoughts and words possess power. We can think ourselves into feeling bad, just as we can think ourselves into feeling good. So today, you will work on becoming aware of your thoughts, and practice thinking yourself into wellness.

Change your way of thinking:
As you wake and prepare to face the day, tell yourself, "I am healthy and strong. My mind, body, and sprit are one with the perfection of the Universal God." Proceed with your normal routine, no matter how you feel, allow the thoughts you have to possess goodness and well-being. Recognize that you are One with our Universal God source, and in Its presence **all** is perfect and

well. Remember that your thoughts have creative power, if you can conceive yourself as having illness, you can create that experience and have it manifest in your reality. Be careful of what you allow yourself to think upon. If illness is not an experience you choose, don't allow yourself to imagine it. Develop a list of positive statements or declarations that you can use to tell yourself how good you feel, and how totally healthy you are.

> This exercise is not to be substituted or replaced with your regular doctor's checkups. You must pay attention to severe health conditions, and take necessary precautions.

When using declarations they should be simple enough for you to remember, and use throughout the day. If you experience a time in the day when you begin to feel low or less energetic, select one of these declarations. "My mind and body are One with the Universal God source", "I claim perfect health", "My thoughts control how I feel", "I am at ease with myself", "I am filled with the love and light of our Universal God source", "My body is strong and healthy", " I create my reality and my reality is that of complete wellness".

If you notice yourself moving away from a state of well-being, put yourself in a quiet zone, and concentrate projecting your thoughts and feelings onto one of your declarations. You may find that you are immediately able to return to that state of well-being. It may take a few minutes, but do not be discouraged, you can achieve that state of well-being. This exercise is meant to help you gain a deeper understanding of just how powerful your mind is, and demonstrate that you have more control over your life than you may realize.

As you become more aware of how powerful your thoughts and feelings are, you will notice how the way you think affects the way you feel, and if you desire good health, and well-being, you will choose your thoughts more wisely.

Conclusion:

The purpose of this exercise is to make you aware of not only how powerful your thoughts are, but also to help make you aware of how you may inadvertently contribute to the illness you experience. When you have specific statements to help change your thoughts it becomes easier to change your mind from negative thoughts to more positive ones.

In your journal make the following entries: Day, Date, Journal Exercise. List the following questions, and take the time to answer them.

- What old thoughts did you release while practicing this exercise?

- What new thoughts and ideas did you gain today, and plan to retain?

- How can this exercise benefit?

- How has gaining this new perspective changed or affected your life?

- How will you apply these new ideas in your life?

Conclude your journal entry with an entry that extends gratitude for the experience and all that you learned as a result of this lesson. Also, make a declaration to continue to experience good health, and sustain it now that you have gained more knowledge and insight about how to do so.

LETTING GO OF FEAR

Stride forward with a firm step knowing with a deep certain inner knowing that you will reach every goal you set for yourself, that you will achieve every aim because you walk without fear."
~Eileen Caddy

Fear is paralyzing! It can prevent you from ever moving forward in life. This prayer is to help you deal with the things in your life that cause you fear. It is to help you understand that you are greater than your fears, and that your fears are an illusion blocking your path, and keeping you from experiencing life as you are intended.

Prayer
As I grow strong with each passing day, I have learned that I can trust the Universe. I know the Universe and all of its goodness surrounds me, and fills me with love and strength. Today I ask for courage to face all the fears that have kept me from experiencing the joyful life I am intended. I ask for courage to look at those things that I am fearful of, and realize their truths. I know that when I face them I must be willing to change the way I view them, and begin to embrace a new vision of them through love. I must replace these thoughts, ideas, and feelings of anger, hate, distrust, resentment, fear, and more with the new thoughts of love which better serve the life I am striving to achieve. I realize that feelings of anger, hate, and resentment are all fear based feelings. I also know that each time I replace

an old fear based thought with one of love, I will rewarded with love from the Universe. I am willing to let go of these old feelings and ideas of fear for they no longer serve me. I know the truth about fear now; it has been brought into the light, and no longer to lurk in the darkness for I can see clearly that I truly have nothing to fear. I have learned that I am never alone, and am always in the presence of our Universal God source. I can accept and experience these new thoughts and feelings of love. I can let go and trust in the power of the Universe because I know I have everything I need within me. I need not carry fear with me any longer as my higher power and inner guide resides where fear once was, and I am learning how to listen to their divine messages. I trust the universe; I surrender to the universe knowing that I create my experiences each day. I make choices in partnership with the most powerful source; therefore nothing can ever harm me. I never need to feel lost or alone as my inner guide divinely guides me, and is ever present always willing to bring me home safely. I now release my old thoughts, feelings, ideas, and beliefs of fear, and crate new ones of love.

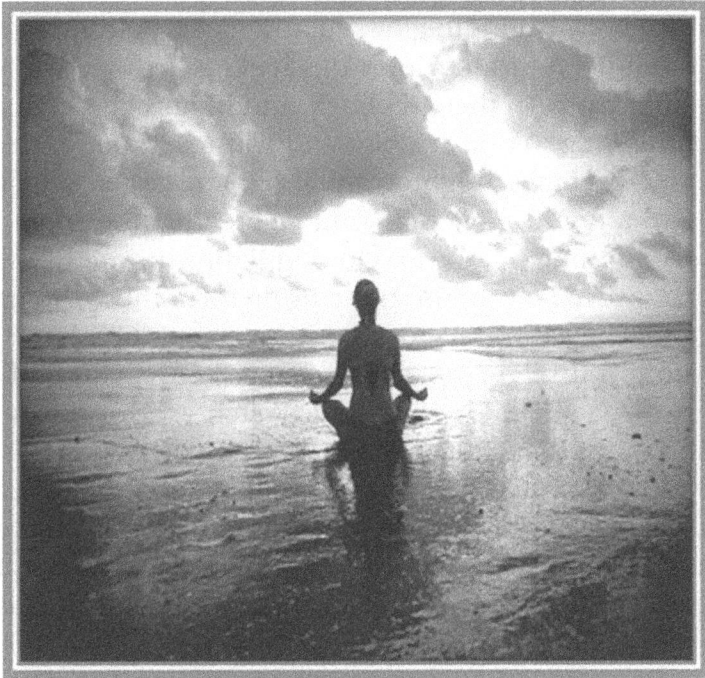

Letting Go of Fear-Meditation

In this meditation you will be asked to face your own personal and inner fears. It is important that you be honest and truthful to yourself about your fear based beliefs and feelings. Here there is no judgment, only love, so whatever your fears are, you can face them safely. Begin by quieting and stilling your mind, surround yourself with things that bring you comfort and security. Think deeply on a time when you felt alone or helpless. Don't worry about the actual outcome of the situation; you are going to create a new, powerful, and happy ending to all those incidents, if you choose. Allow yourself to view these feelings of loneliness, fear, anger, resentment, or jealously, whatever they are. Now, in the midst of all these feelings, imagine warmth beginning to surround you. Imagine this warmth entering your body beginning in your feet, and moving slowly up your legs and entering your entire body. In fact, notice that it begins to extend beyond your body and continues to fill the room you are in. As this warmth comforts you, notice the glow you begin to have. Imagine that your entire body begins to glow, emitting a warm inner light that comes from deep within. Enjoy this feeling, indulge yourself in this feeling, bathe in these feelings, and light. Imagine that this light is pulsating and as it does, and with each pulse, the light within you becomes brighter and brighter, larger, and larger, growing to a point of strength and beauty that the room seems filled with nothing but warm, glowing light with you in the middle of it. Now, in your mind, try to bring forth those thoughts or feelings that cause you to fear, be it a person, a place or something. Allow yourself to see it, just see it. Notice it's insignificance in the presence of this warm light. Watch as it dissolves like a spark in front of you. Allow each fear to experience this same mini explosion until all of your fears appear and then disappear like sparks lighting up and then going out. Do this until all the fears you can think of spark out. Enjoy the firework show as your fears spark and disappear right in front of you. As the last fear sparks out, you begin to realize the intense feeling that this warm light has left you with. You realize that it is pure love. The room and you are filled with the light, the warmth, the energy of pure love. You realize that you did nothing to cause the fears to spark out except expose them to the light of pure love. Remain in the warm glowing room for as long as you like experiencing yourself in the cleansing effect of this light that is pure love. When you are ready to leave the room, simply feel the pulses again, and let each pulse cause the light to become dimmer bit by bit, and begin to turn down the warmth until you see and feel yourself in the room again.

Remember:
This can be a very powerful exercise in assisting you with learning to control the energy within you. Your discovery of being able to generate light can be used to embrace or dispel many different things. When you are in the presence of this light, know that only love can exist there. No thought other than love can survive in the room of light filled with love. You may want to use this meditation many times to experience this feeling or to release

stress or anger as it arises in your life, or as fear attempts to creep back into your mind.

Each time you experience this meditation, you should feel more and more filled with love. The stronger you become, the longer the experience should sustain you.

Affirmations for letting go of Fear

- "I have learned to walk without fear as I know my Universal God source is always with me."

- "I am a powerful being. There is only one thing greater than me, and I have nothing to fear."

- "I have all I need to unlock the chains that fear has kept me bound with."

Journal Exercise for Letting go of Fear

You have made it this far not because you are without fear but because you have already chosen courage over fear. Congratulations! You have made a very wise choice, one that will allow you to continue to move forward towards your life changing experiences. There are many things in life that may cause you fear, but what you forget is that it is only in your mind that fear can enter your life. If you do not choose to experience fear, it has no entrance into your life. Some people say that fear is a good thing because it works as an alarm system to alert you, and helps keep you safe from things that could harm you. In my experience fear has never been a good thing, it has always kept me from the things I want most, and it has been our Universal God source that has kept me from harm, not fear.

Letting go of fear can be a very fearful experience within itself. Many of you have learned how to tolerate fear to some degree, and work with it in your lives every day. You may have learned to use fear to keep from doing things you are uncomfortable with or it may have kept you from learning things you didn't want to understand. You may have turned to fear to keep from dealing with things that are too unpleasant for you to deal with. Some of you may have even become comfortable with the feeling of fear, believing if fear isn't present there must be something really wrong, or something to really be fearful of. Believe it or not, many of you have become comfortable with feeling fearful; in some cases fear can become as close to you as a best friend. In this instance, choosing to remain fearful will keep you from experiencing life as you are intended. It can cause you to look away from the truth. It can cause you to walk past gifts that are brought to you from the Universe. It will cause you to close your mind to thoughts and beliefs that can free you. But you will work on dealing with all the things fear affects so that you can see clearly what you are missing, and know that you have "nothing to fear but fear itself".

Today in your journal you will be writing a resignation letter, resigning yourself from all your fears. Think of this exercise as though you are resigning from a job that no longer suits you, and you are moving on to one that offers better opportunities for growth, experience, and greater compensation. If you knew that by resigning from your fears you could receive these benefits, I'm sure you would have very little trouble with letting go, right? But, just in case you're still having trouble letting go, think of this. If you remain in your current fearful position, you will not only receive a cut in pay, but a demotion with no potential for advancement at all. Does that make it a bit easier to let go of fear? In your current position, fear wants you to work hard for no pay! Before you begin your resignation letter, create a list of all the things about this current "position" or job, (Your fears), that you want to resign from. Also, write down what you would rather experience instead, i.e.:

List of fears you want to resign from/experiences I would rather choose

- I'm afraid of being alone, and I choose to experience a loving and compassionate relationship.

- I'm afraid of feeling that I don't have enough money, I choose to feel abundant.

- I'm afraid of life going on without me; I would rather experience myself being a part of new and fun situations.

- There is no opportunity for growth, and I'm afraid that my life is going nowhere; I choose to have more fun and joy in my life.

- I have no health benefits, and I'm afraid that my illness will get worse; I choose to be fit and have good health.

- I'm worried about not having a place to live; I choose to have a permanent, safe residence for me and my family.

Whatever your fears, write them down specifically, its' very important to address all of them so don't e afraid or leave anything out. After the list is complete, begin your letter by making sure you list the date, address it to: Dear Fears. Create sentences that say: "I am resigning from... (List your fears), "I no longer want to be afraid of"... "Being afraid of... keeps me from being able to...", "I no longer want to be afraid of..., I now choose...", "I do not enjoy being afraid to..., I would rather experience...". In each sentence that you list a fear, make sure you add to that sentence what it is you choose to experience that is different from those feelings of fear.

Example: **Letter of Resignation**
Date:
Dear Fears:
I am resigning from my fears, and am choosing courage in its place. I have been afraid of the experience of lack or of not having enough, and now I choose to have a life of abundance. I choose to move from this state of mind because it has made me feel afraid of not being able to support my family although I choose to make a living that will sustain a comfortable lifestyle. I choose to resign because the lifestyle I'm leading is causing me to always be afraid of getting sick and not feeling well, and what I choose is to feel healthy, strong, and fit. I have been afraid of being alone, but now

I know that I am worthy of a loving companion therefore I chose to have happiness, and a loving individual in my life. I no longer want to feel afraid of not having a place to live; I desire a permanent residence in an area that is safe for me and my children with a park and school that will support our spiritual growth. I no longer want to feel afraid of my friends having a better life than me as I choose to have a life with no worries, full of joy, and enjoyment. Being afraid of not having what I want in life keeps me from growing, and I choose to be with people who love so that I can enjoy the kind of life that keeps me strong, happy, joyful, and loving. I'm letting go of all my fears so that I can move towards the life I choose for myself. I look forward to all the possibilities offered by our Universal God source, and I am thankful for the coming opportunities to help me create my life as I choose it to be.

Happily,

After you have completed your letter, read it out loud. Read it with courage, knowing that you are putting all your fears behind you. If after you have read it out loud, and realize that you'd like to add more, do so. Be specific, and detailed, put all your fears behind you. Now, seal and address the letter to our Universal God source at My Universe, USA, zip code – 0000, the return address will be from you with your name, address, city, state, and zip code.

Now, say this prayer: **"Universal God, enclosed, and sealed in this envelope is my letter of resignation acknowledging that I am letting go of all my fears. I realize that these fears have kept me from experiencing happiness, good health, and prosperity as I am intended. I have chosen to replace my fears with courage and faith and want to leave behind all doubt and worry. I cast these fears into the Universe and know they will not return to me unless I choose them to. I choose a relationship with our Universal God source that will sustain that which I have chosen to enhance my life, and extend love and gratitude for all that I will soon receive. I know I have the power to choose only the experiences which will bring me closer to the power in the Universe, and help me reach my higher self and greater good."** Thank you.

Conclusion

You have created a very powerful message that states that you have put your trust and faith in our Universal God source, allowing your fears to be eternally sealed. You need never open the letter you just created, and know that you need not face those fears again, unless you choose to. You made a decision that your life would be more beneficial without fear and in doing so you are creating your life anew.

Next Important Step... Gratitude Letter

Just as you have created a resignation letter, resigning from your fears, it is also important to create a letter that gives thanks for that which you are expecting to receive. When creating the resignation letter you also made specific choices of what you would choose to put in the place of fear. Your next important step will be to create a Gratitude letter where you list all that which you have to be grateful for. You will not only list that which you now have but also that which you asked for because you know it is on its way to you. Let's give thanks for what you anticipate receiving as well.

Begin the same as with the resignation letter. Prepare a list of all the things in your life you feel grateful for. You can choose how extensive the list is but make sure to list significant things as well as some of the things you may feel are insignificant because there is much that we all have to feel grateful for.

Example of Gratitude letter:
Date:
Dear Universal God Source:

This is a letter of gratitude. I want to extend thanks to all the things in my life I have been gifted with. I am thankful that I have the strength, and abilities to prepare this letter. I am thankful for the fact that I have awakened to see yet another beautiful day. Thank you for my home, it is stable, permanent, and safe. It provides me warmth, shelter, and security. I have all the things in my home to provide me with comfort. I am also grateful for my job. It allows me to earn a living that helps me support my family.

It provides me the opportunities that will allow me to grow and advance professionally. I appreciate and am thankful for my reliable transportation without it; it would be much more difficult for me to do the things I need to do each day. I am thankful for the friends and family that are in my life.

With love and support I am able to experience counsel, guidance, and support......

In Anticipation

(your name)

Continue on with your letter to include all that you feel thankful for. Remember, it is important to include those things you listed in your letter of resignation as your new choices to replace fear. It may be a little difficult for you to imagine those things you don't recognize in your reality at this time but if you cannot imagine yourself with them, you will be without them. You must be able to visualize yourself actually in receipt of all your choices, its part of the process of creating these experiences. Complete the same process by reading the letter out loud. Allowing yourself to hear what it is you have to be thankful for is very important. Allow yourself to experience the feelings in your letter, the excitement, joy, safety, security, whatever the feelings are, allow them, and remember them. Think about them frequently which will help you easily experience gratitude.

After you have completed the letter seal and address it to our Universal God source, for example at "My Universe, USA, zip code – 0000", the return address will be from you with your name, address, city, state, and zip code.

After you have completed the letter end it by reciting this prayer:

"Thank you for all things in my life. I extend gratitude and appreciation for all the gifts I have received. These gifts allow me to live a full life. They bring me peace, security, and joy, they offer me happiness, and comfort. These gifts help me remember who I really am and allow me to experience myself as One with the power in the Universe. This relationship is of the greatest importance to me for without this connection, I am powerless. I

appreciate my new found knowledge as it allows me to create my world as I would have it, and experience the joys of life that will enable me to soar. Thank you for the peace, love, good health, clarity, courage, and forgiveness I have received. These gifts will enhance my life and allow me to live the life I am intended."
Thank You

(Feel free to compose a letter that you are comfortable with, and one that lists the specific things in your life that you are thankful for. The purpose of the letter is to extend gratitude, and it can be composed in any form that suits you).

Conclusion

In this exercise you have created a very powerful message that states that you have put your trust in our Universal God source, allowing your fears to be eternally sealed. You need never open the letter you just created knowing that you have already faced those fears, and need not face them again, unless you choose to. You made a decision that your life would be more beneficial without fear, and in doing so you are creating your life anew. In your journal record and answer the following questions:

- How easy was it for you to face your fears?

- How did you feel resigning from them?

- What were the 3 greatest fears to resign from, and why?

- How will your life be impacted now that you no longer have to be fearful?

- What will make it difficult for you not to look back on to your fears?

- How will you deal with those difficulties?

- What changes will you be able to make in your life as a result of your resignation of fear?

- How has your perspective changed as a result of your resignation?

Conclude your journal entry with a declaration of letting go of fear, and record all that you learned as a result of this exercise. Also make a declaration to continue to allow yourself to remain fearless now that you have replaced fear with courage and faith.

Discard your letter in any manner you wish, bury it, burn it or throw it in the garbage. Whatever you choose, remove it from your presence as you have decided to rid yourself of the fears sealed within it!

OVERCOMING LOSS

**So, live that when the summons comes to join the innumerable
caravan, which moves to that mysterious realm where each shall
take His chamber in the silent halls of death, thou go not like
the quarry-slave at night, scourged to his dungeon, but sustained and soothed by an unfaltering trust, approach thy grave,
like one who wraps the drapery of his couch about him,
and lies down to pleasant dreams.**
~ William Cullen Bryant

There are times in our lives when we all experience the loss of a
love one or of someone close to us. It could be the loss of a loved
one, a friend, a companion pet, and the lonely feelings that come
from that loss can feel overwhelming. This prayer and exercise will
help you realize that you are not alone, and give you strength to look
beyond the pain the feeling of loss often leaves you with.

Prayer

As I enter this prayer my heart is heavy and sad, and filled with
grief of my loss. I feel empty and alone and I pray for a way to
heal from this loss. I pray to replace the emptiness within my
heart with love and joy which I once felt.

I find it hard to face each day but I know that in order to get past
these feelings I must look to each day with great anticipation of the
experiences that lay before me. I know that I must see each experience as an opportunity to show love and gratitude for all things
and all circumstances. I am learning to accept the knowledge that

in life there will be loved ones that leave this physical realm and will return to our Universal God source. That source is the mind of God, a place where we are never forgotten or loss, the place from which we all originated, and will return. I am seeking peace with the knowledge that the loss that I am experiencing is that of their physical body, not of their spirit. Their spirit will always be with me. I am grateful that my loved one has been released from the burden of their body, and is whole again and in the presence of God. The love that I have for those who have departed and the love that they have for me lives on; they have not died, they have simply moved to another place in time to serve a deeper purpose. I accept that their leaving is only because their work here has ended, and they are now embarking upon a new journey of ultimate love, and I am thankful for the time we shared our lives together. I have been left with loving memories and wonderful experiences that will allow me to keep the love for them always in my heart. I pray for strength to move on and continue to seek joy in my life. For every time I experience joy I will remember them as they brought me so much of it. I pray for their journey home, and know that they will be received with love. I also know that at the time I cross over we shall meet again.

Overcoming Loss Meditation

Let us begin this meditation by finding a quiet place to sit and relax. In this meditation, it might be helpful to find an object to concentrate on. It could be a flower in a vase or the leaf of a plant or even the flicker of a candle. Whatever you choose, make it your focus of attention. In this space first acknowledge all of the sounds that you hear, and then gently let those sounds evaporate and disappear. Relax your body from the tips of your toes to the top of your head.

Take several deep cleansing breaths as you visualize yourself at the seashore on a clear beautiful day, with a gentle wind blowing across the waters. Imagine that you have in your hand a string that is attached to a beautiful red balloon; full of helium and anxious to fly. See the string as it pulls taunt in your fist, and you pull back, not wanting to lose the beautiful balloon. As you grasp tightly, the tug of war between the wind wanting to cast the balloon into the skies, and you wanting it to remain safely within your hand until the balloon is caught up in a strong updraft, yanks the string from your hand. The balloon momentarily drifts and dips overhead as if saying its goodbye, gently at first, and then gleefully drifts from sight. You know that its beauty and energy is now headed in a new direction, and while you feel a bit sad that it has left you, you realize that while you had it by the string it filled you with love and laughter, and you feel gratitude for that. Acknowledge the feeling of loss as you look out at the clouds no longer able to see the balloon. Imagine that you continue walking down the beach pondering your loss, but knowing that we all have a destiny to fulfill, and also know that when the time to part arrives there is always sadness but that sadness is not meant to remain with you. The memories of love, joy, excitement, and gratitude are what is meant to remain, and remember that the spirit also remains with you always. Make a vow that your journey will be filled with as much fun, joy, and love as the balloon that drifted away.

Affirmations for Overcoming Loss

- "I release those I have loved and learned from, knowing that they are in a better place."

- "There is no such experience of loss, our spirits are eternal and last forever, they never pass away."

- "Our Universal God source wants me to live the best life I am intended, and to do that I must live with feelings joy not sadness or loss."

Journal Exercise for Overcoming Loss
Today is a day to acknowledge, and honor the loss of a special part of you. In every one's life, at one time or another, we will experience what we perceive as a loss. Everyone will experience pain of this "loss", and of not having that special companion here with you. But, what is often not realized is that nothing and no one is ever lost to us, ever! To lose something implies that you are without it. Through the knowledge that we are not only connected, but we are an eternal part of everything and everyone in the Universe, proves that we can never be separated from each other. The reality is that your loved ones are not lost, but that they are no longer in your physical presence. You can no

longer touch, feel, physically see and interact with them physically. However, their spiritual presence is part of the Universe, making it impossible for you to ever be without them. The other reason you can never be without them is because they are part of creation, part of our experiences. Yes, you co-created this companion, this relationship, this special bond, this eternal connection. Your desire to give love, share love, and to be in love is part of what caused this manifestation of your relationship with them in the first place. In fact, you have not ever lost love, for you are love and it is also always within you. It is the absence of that special one that causes the sadness that is felt. Your memory of that special one's spirit has caused a longing for their presence. What you must learn is how to connect with them on a different level. You must learn how to create that loving memory within your spirit, and be satisfied with it there.

In this exercise you will reestablish that presence that is so missed. You will do this by first learning to crate symbolisms of their absence. You will learn to recreate their spiritual presence. You may have already memorialized this companion through traditional means, by way of a funeral, memorial service or some other form of honor. In order to recreate the spiritual presence let us first acknowledge the connection. Today in your journal you will dedicate special time to re-member (reconnect) with this companion, meaning you will become a member with them again.

Begin your journal entry by entering the date, day, time, and heading of "exercise on Loss". Write down the name of the special one you want to reconnect with. Complete the full exercise for each special one you choose to reconnect with. Begin to write down all your memories of this special one. Write about their personality, their gifts, their quirks, how they made you feel, what made them unique, what made them silly. Write all that you can remember about them, and your relationship with them.

- Write about what made them so special to you. In as much detail as possible, describe the relationship.

- Write about how it feels to be without them, what that relationship brought to your life, how they or it impacted your life.

- Write about what you miss most about that companionship.

As you write, allow yourself to experience the feelings you are having right now. In spite of the pain, try to stay with your feelings, and memories. Cry, shout, whatever feelings come, allow yourself to release them. Write for as long as you like, write about anything you remember of your special one.

Once you feel you have written your deepest feelings, close your journal, and put it away for a day or two. If you feel the need to go back to it and write more, do so but try not to move past where you are right now. Now, think about a special item that may have belonged to that special one that brings you joy, or it may have brought them joy. It doesn't have to be something that actually belonged to that special one, if you have something that belonged to them directly, use it. If not think of that special something as a symbol, and use it. For example if your special one loved gardening, pick up a pack of seeds of their favorite plant. If you special one loved to wear a special pair of socks, pick up a pair of socks in their favorite color or favorite material. Just think of something that will allow you to think on them with happiness. Keep it simple, use that special something that holds significant meaning to you or them, a picture, memento, a piece of clothing or an article that you both loved together. Think on how this article was used by this special one. It may have been a shirt or favorite pair of shoes or the car keys they could never keep up with. If your special one was a companion pet, that article may be their color or leash or the label from the can of their favorite treat or food. You may have a special photograph of the two of you doing something funny or special. Whatever it is, gather it, bring it out from the hiding place you may have put it. Just that single something, no need to unpack all of their belongings. Now, place that item in its natural place. Where ever it was when you shared it with your special one, place it back in its place. If that item was a set of keys to their favorite car, hang them where they used to be. If it was a collar or leash, place it near the area it was kept. The point of this exercise is to reestablish the spiritual presence of your special one. We are working towards reestablishing the connection you feel you have lost. Once the item is placed back in its natural place, it creates a symbol of their presence. As it is placed in its setting, make the following claim, **"As this item only symbolizes your presence, I feel connected to it. As I place this item here in its natural place, it helps me remember the natural place you eternally hold in my soul, therefore, as I know it is here, I know that you are ever present within my life. I honor our connection, knowing that you are eternally with me."**

Because you know that you are part of everything in the Universe, you know that your special one remains a part of you. You may not only visit your memories of them, but you may acknowledge their spiritual presence whenever you desire. This exercise is only one way for you to remember their presence, you may think of other ways that are better suited for you. This exercise can also be used to recreate or reestablish a connection with a special one you may not have been close to or near at their passing. You can recreate the connection you wished you would have had by using this exercise and symbolism to represent the relationship you were working to achieve, or wished you had achieved. You are in control of the positive memories and connection you choose to establish.

As time passes and you become stronger and able to acknowledge your connection, you may not feel the need to use the item or article to symbolize their spiritual presence. You will eventually know that it is so, and be able to draw up an image or feelings that will allow you to experience that connection. Everyone grieves differently; there is no way to calculate how much time an individual may need for grief to lessen. Many people are able to move beyond the pair when they are able to understand the idea of Oneness with our Universal God source. When you recognize that you are never alone or without any one you may be able to restore your feelings of loss immediately, but there is no rush.

It must be done in your own time, and on your terms. Simply remember that your feelings of loss can be restored once you understand that you are part of everything, and you are less likely to feel alone or disconnected from your special one.

Conclusion

The idea of this exercise is to acknowledge the relationship in a happy and positive way which can be done by writing about the relationship, and then to allow yourself to reconnect to those special memories and feelings. Traditionally it is natural to feel that you have lost this special one because their physical manifestation is no longer present for you to see, touch, or physically interact with. Remember, the spiritual connection can never be lost.

Conclude your journal entry with an entry that extends your gratitude for the connection, and experience you shared with this special one. Include al that you have learned as a result of this experience.

ACHIEVING CLARITY

"The best and most beautiful things in the world cannot be seen or even heard, but must be felt with the heart."
~Helen Keller

This prayer will remind you to focus your attention on what it is that you desire for your life, not on what you do not desire.

Prayer
I choose clarity as it will enable me to see beauty and love in every situation I choose clarity so that I may achieve a higher degree of understanding of all that is in the world around me. Clarity will help me choose the perfect experiences for my journey. Clarity will not allow me to be clouded by reflections of the past or longings for the future. It will allow me to gain better focus so that I may be more specific in creating my desires. I embrace clarity with divine love and acceptance and I am grateful for all of the possibilities it offers me. With clarity I intend to be clearer in my thoughts and my desires. Clarity will allow me to be more confident in the steps I take each day. It will help me realize my purpose and recognize the gifts given me by our Universal God source. It will allow me to remain focused upon those things that are positive and good, and help me utilize all that I receive for the betterment of myself and mankind.

Achieving Clarity Meditation

It is very important for this meditation to first empty your mind of all the distractions of the day. So, take time to find that quite space in your mind as you begin to relax and filter out the noises around you. Take several deep cleansing breaths. With the release of each breath, release old thoughts, and with each breath in, bring in the clarity.

During this meditation you will be working to imagine that you are in the woods on a beautiful clear day. Imagine that you are sitting beside a stream of crystal clear water. As you gaze down into the clear water you are able to see the smooth rocks that line the bottom of the stream. Imagine that you are able to hear the clear water gently rushing over the smooth rocks, and as you do, feel the slight breeze in the air as the trees lining the bank bend and sway ever so slightly as though dancing with the wind. Imagine that the sounds around you grow louder as you listen to the tinkle and trickle of the stream very clearly as it moves lazily along. Notice that there is nothing you need to for the stream to flow along. There is nothing you need to do to see the clarity of the water, but to focus your gaze. Gaze deeper into the stream and allow the water to bring you clarity. As you gain this deeper clarity, allow yourself to see your reflection. In this reflection imagine that you are happy, healthy, successful, prosperous, and surrounded by loved ones full of joy. Remain with those thoughts and feelings for a while. See yourself with good health. See yourself successful at the work you do. See yourself prosperous, enjoying your abundance. Feel the feelings that these images cause you to have. Now look around you at the trees with their branches and limbs hanging overhead. Notice that hanging from their branches are all the things you desire in life, just waiting for you to pluck them from the branch, and enjoy their goodness.

As you look again into the stream and see yourself enjoying each desire, continue to hold the vision for as long as you can; seeing whatever it is that you plucked from the trees. Think on these desires deeply, for your thoughts have creative power! As you imagine yourself enjoying the desires, think on what feelings these visions cause you to have. Allow yourself to feel the joy, excitement, contentment and fulfillment they offer. Expect that your desires will manifest in your life just as easily as the water flowing down the stream. Know they will arrive. **KNOW IT TO BE SO!** Now offer thanks to our Universal God source.

Remember
It is not easy to let go and "go with the flow." Often we want to do something to help ourselves. But in life's stream, the more you try to "help", the more you can get in the way. More often than not your attempts to help may create WAVES, interfering with the natural flow of the stream. The best thing we can do for ourselves when we have desires is to **believe,** and then let go. Act as though you have this desire, allow yourself to be excited about it. Allow yourself to experience the feelings you would have if that desire were in your life today. That's what it means to "let go". Let

our Universal God source bring it to you, you simply enjoy, and know that it is on its way!

Affirmations on Achieving Clarity

- "My thoughts, feelings, and desires are clear."

- "Clarity helps me focus so that I clearly manifest the desires is I choose."

- "My mind is calm and serene this gives me a clear focus and a centered perspective."

- "My feelings are clear to me. I understand and accept them, and use them to help create my greater good."

- "All that I see is part of me, I choose to see, and experience love, peace, and joy."

Journal Exercise for Achieving Clarity

Today we will work on helping you learn to focus and remove the distractions that block you from seeing, and experiencing life clearly.

The first step in gaining clarity is to acknowledge that you do not have a clear picture of how you would like to see your life at this time. Begin the day by declaring that you choose to see more clearly than you ever have before.

Consciously plan to take your time as you move through your day at a much slower pace than usual. Tell yourself to pay attention, as there are messages from the Universe delivered to you throughout the day that you may not often see or receive. These messages act as guides or road signs that will bring you closer to what it is you choose to experience. Today you've chosen to experience Clarity so slow down, and focus.

Exercise 1

Make a list of all the things you could do to help you gain more clarity. The list could look like this:

1. Slow down
2. Pay attention
3. Listen deeply
4. Live in the moment
5. Smile before talking
6. Turn down or off the radio or television for a couple of hours
7. Be more aware of the people around me
8. Make a conscious effort to look at everyone that crosses my path
9. Talk a walk in nature by yourself. Take time out for just me

Once you have made your list, transfer each suggestion onto a single sticky note or colorful piece of paper. Using brightly colored ink or markers, print each one large enough to further catch your attention. Place these clarity notes somewhere where you will see them at least once a day for the next three days. The trick to this exercise is rid your mind of all the clutter that prevents you from focusing on positive thoughts, feelings and emotions. Whenever you can fill your mind with good, positive thoughts, you will begin to cancel out old habits, and patterns of negative thinking. Your positive thoughts, feelings, and emotions have creative power. They help you gain a clearer picture of what it is you desire, and how to begin to create it. Also, focusing in this manner allows you to be conscious, aware, and more in control of what you are thinking, and feeling. This conscious way of thinking enables you to control your feelings, and allows you to generate more positive energy to focus towards your desires which puts you in a much better position to begin creating your desires.

Exercise 2
In this exercise, pick several things you may have wanted to do the day before or the week before, but did not or could not take the time to do them. Select at least three things that you can commit yourself to do sometime within the next three days. Make sure it is something that you can do reasonably like make an overdue

phone call, e-mail a message to a friend, go to the library o book store, or stop by the nursery and pick up a plant.

The idea is to identify what it is you wish to do or accomplish, and commit to doing it and keep it focused in your mind; no matter how small it seems, until you actually accomplish the task. While you are completing these tasks, think about how they have allowed you to redirect your focus. Offer gratitude to them for allowing you to focus more on getting clear in your thoughts and intentions. After you have completed each task, allow yourself to experience the accomplishment of actually doing it. By allowing yourself this extra time, you are also confirming your commitment to what it is you are asking for, which is to slow down enough to gain clarity. This is also a great exercise to rid yourself of procrastination as well. We tend to procrastinate when we feel overwhelmed, when we are distracted, and when we don't allow ourselves to focus on the small things.

The second part of this exercise is to begin to pay closer attention to you. Notice all the wonderful things about you, and take the time to say them out loud, and then write them down in your journal. For example say out loud, "today I notice how rested I feel and look", or "today I notice how good I feel wearing this outfit:, "I am proud of myself for taking the time to work on gaining clarity", "whatever it is that you want to acknowledge about yourself that you would have otherwise not noticed and acknowledged. You can extend this exercise by making notice of a subject or even that you are involved in frequently, but have paid little attention to. In other words, things you may be taking for granted. Slow down, gain focus, and observe this "thing". Think about how having more information and clarity about it could benefit you.

Conclusion

These exercises are about taking steps that will allow you to gain more clarity. Some of the steps are to slow down, gain focus, take notice or observe, and pay attention. Determine the results of this process. Ask yourself how becoming clearer has benefited you. As you complete the exercise take the time to journal your experiences. Make sure you record all the things you have done, and what you have learned from them. Record and answer the following questions:

- How has gaining clarity helped you?

- In what ways can this be used to help you crate your desires?

- What will you do differently tomorrow that you did not do today?

- Write about how this experience affected your perspective.

- What was the most important experience you had during the three days you worked on gaining clarity, and why?

- Conclude your journal entry with a statement that extends gratitude from the experience, and all that you learned as a result of your experience.

- Also make a declaration to continue to hold clarity now that you have found a way to claim it.

ONENESS WITH OUR UNIVERSAL GOD

"I would rather walk in the dark with God (the Universe) than walk alone in the light."
~Mary Gardiner Brainard

This prayer will remind you that you are never alone; our Universal God source is always with you. You are One with our Universal God source, the greatest power in the entire Universe.

Prayer

I give thanks for arriving at the realization that I am one with the greatest power in the Universe. I am one with all that is and I am never alone while on this journey. I am part of a collective consciousness one that surrounds our entire Universe with unconditional love, and it is through this love that I am now free to experience all that I choose for my life. In choosing my desires I am aware of the unity that exists between every living entity on our planet and I am filled with gratitude for the honor of being at one with it.

I come with a grateful heart, knowing that as I enter into partnership with our Universal God source, I am transformed. I have awakened to the knowledge that with Universal God as my partner I can create a new life with new thoughts, feelings, and ideas about who I really am. I now release all the past thoughts about myself and the world that for they have not served me well. These thoughts of lack, doubt, fear or powerlessness are no longer part of my reality. I am One with the greatest power in the Universe.

I begin this journey with a new realization that I am not alone in this vast and endless Universe, and I have the power to choose what I desire to experience here on earth. I feel the power and unconditional love within me, and recognize it as a part of me. I know that I am connected to the Omnipresence of Universal God. I recognize Universal God as complete love, therefore, I am love, and I demonstrate that love to the Universe by loving myself unconditionally. I am thankful for the realization of my divine partnership with our Universal God, and of my knowledge that I can do all things, achieve all goals, and can live my life to the fullest in complete joy and happiness. I have the power to change those things in my life that I no longer choose to experience.

Oneness with Our Universal God Meditation
Find a comfortable, quiet place to sit and relax. Visualize your-self being in the most peaceful surroundings that you can think of; on the seashore or sitting on a rock overlooking the ocean. Wherever you envision peace, even if you have never been there before, take your mind to that place. Visualize the feelings of the peace this place brings you. Hold the ideas, feelings, and thoughts of peace in your mind. Allow yourself to feel the relaxation you feel. For the next few moments take in the sounds around you. Listen to the sounds and then let them go as we begin to take your peace to another place.

Take three deep cleansing breaths, and relax your body. In your mind visualize taking a walk in the forest along a path filled with the fallen leaves of the trees. As you continue down the path, see a small whirlwind of leaves being picked up by a swirl of soft, warm wind. As you watch this sight, imagine that you see yourself as one of those leaves. Notice that the wind moves in a circular motion picking up more and re leaves. Envision the circle growing larger and larger, notice that the leaves are being transformed into sparks of light as the circle moves faster and faster in motion. As the leaves begin to pick up speed visualize them as they are lifted further off the forest floor and begin to raise above all the tall trees. See the circle now extend and rise reaching beyond the sky. Imagine that the force of what was leaves continue to spark and swirl and encircle the globe, always remaining peaceful, warm, and safe. As you visualize more you realize that what was once individual sparks of light have now joined together in one continuous circle of light, and you are part of that light that becomes more and more brilliant. You begin to feel a part of this continuous light. You can feel the warmth of it, the power of it, and the peace of it. You now feel the Oneness of it as together you move towards an even brighter light that emits an overwhelming feeling of peace and love such that you have never experienced. You long to join deeper with this light of Oneness, and as you do the circle lingers momentarily soaking up all of the peaceful and healing light, absorbing all the love of our Universal God. Slowly the circle begins to move again, gently returning through atmosphere, returning to earth, through the skies, and back to the forest from where it originated. The circle of light slows in motion returning to leaves and moving closer to the forest floor where each leaf is placed back upon the ground and where you awaken feeling renewed, and at peace with the knowledge that you are now truly one with our Universal God source.

Remember
Every thought you have has an impact upon the Universe because you are One, we are One with It. You must be mindful of your thoughts; for it is through your thoughts and beliefs that your desires are propelled through the Universe and back to you carrying the manifestation of your desires.

Affirmations of Oneness

- "I am One with our Universal God source"

- "I am One in the light, One in the love, and One in the power of Universal God"

- "The power of Universal God lies within me"

Journal Exercise for Achieving Oneness with Our Universal God
Today is a day to celebrate! For you have reached a point in this live changing journey where you realize that there is a connection between you and our Universal God source. You have learned about the power of thought, you have chosen to embrace our source of love, you have declared your strength, and have declared yourself worthy of all that the Universal has to offer. Today you will begin to experience the divine connection between you and our Universal God source.

This connection is not limited to only our Universal God source; it is a connection to and with everything in the entire Universe. Take a moment and allow your mind to wrap itself around that idea. Yes, it's true; you are connected to everything, everyone, and everything in this Universe. If that is so, and it is, that makes you far greater than you ever imagined, and you are! You, or who you really are is greater than your body, you are greater than other peoples images of you, you are even greater than the image you have of yourself. What you really are is Love, love is all and everything you are. It is what you are here to experience, unless you choose not to, but even if you choose not to be **love,** you truly can be nothing else. You can experience yourself being without love but even then, in that experience you are still Love. How awesome is that? Just as our universal God is Love, so is it that you are also! You and our Universal God source entered into a sort of "agreement" together to have the experiences you are now having. You agreed to participate in what is an illusion of separation from our Universal God source temporarily in order to have the experiences of your choice.

A temporary illusion not separated from or disconnected from, as you could never be disconnected from Universal God. This illusion is pretty unique because it is only temporary, and you can be aware of it or it can remain an illusion if you choose. It's true that it's pretty difficult to see through the illusion especially if you're not paying attention or if you choose not to believe it. But the point is that it is your choice, it is completely up to you to decide or chose to participate in this illusion in whatever way you choose. The problem is that most people don't know they even have a choice so they remain convinced of the illusion of separation which causes them much pain and confusion.

This agreement is necessary in order to create the experiences you would choose for yourself. If you remained with our Universal God, and only knew yourself as God, you could never experience yourself as YOU. It was necessary to create a way for you to experience you without being Universal God in order to have the experiences you choose. This completely unselfish act has allowed each and every one of us to experience free will, to choose what it is we want to do, be, have, and create. This act of free will allows us to create an unlimited amount of experiences, in fact there is no experience that you cannot have, and there will never be a time that you will be denied an experience. You have been given complete and free will to choose all of your life's experience. It's like being in an unlimited candy story with every type of candy you can imagine. What's awesome is that the candy counter helper is our Universal God who is always available to scoop out your choice or experience while you stand at the glass counter pointing at your next choice, co crating your experience together. Each time you change your mind about the choice of candy you desire a new selection or experience is offered. If you're not satisfied with that choice, chose again, and again, and again, if you chose.

This idea may be completely new to you, or it may be one you've struggled to believe but want it to be so. In this exercise you will have an opportunity to create an "agreement" between you and our Universal God source that is important to you. When creating this "agreement" there is key information you may want to be aware of to assure that you are working towards creating your greater good, and you actually are working to create the desires you choose. The reason this information is important is because the point of creating this agreement is to also help you understand the appropriate frame of mind you should be in while you are creating your agreement. For example, if you don't believe any of this is possible, you will not be as successful as you would be if you had true faith and conviction of its possibilities. Also if you write your agreement and it is filled with doubt, fear, or negative idea and thoughts, that's exactly what you will create, an agreement filled with negative thoughts, ideas, and experiences. We've taken the time to offer you a few suggestions but remember this is your agreement, and you will get out of it what you put into it. Here is a list of some of the things you may want to include in your agreement:

- Believe that what you agree to is possible

- Prepare your agreement with confidence

- Allow yourself to have good feelings about this agreement

- Get excited

- Expect to receive what you request or desire

- Everything on the contract should be positive

- Your "wants" should be desires. If you say you want something you're telling the Universe to bring you experiences that make you "want", not bring you experiences of what you desire

- Be clear in what it is you desire (clarity)

- Write you agreement with expectation, knowing it will be given, knowing that it is already in the Universe waiting for you

- Be specific about what it is you desire

- Don't be afraid to ask, fear is not positive. Fear only brings more fear

Let's begin your agreement. Begin to create in your mind thoughts of images that you would like to experience. Also, be sure to add positive declarations that will acknowledge your connection.

Example of Universal Agreement
I acknowledge and embrace my full connection and Oneness with our Universal God source. I enter into this agreement of Love with Universal God knowing that I AM part of all things. I choose to always be aware of my connection, and always know myself as One. The love of our Universal God allows me to declare that "I AM Love", "I AM goodness", "I AM light", "I AM creative energy". "I AM a kind and loving mother, wife, and friend". "I AM able to share my love with all who are around me unselfishly". "I will continue to live my life in the presence of our Universal God, and share everything that I AM with others". "I choose to be healthy so that I may live a vibrant life". "I choose to experience happiness in the work that I do, and I agree to appreciate the blessing of joyful employment." "In my life I choose to experience joy in my relationships, and I agree to love and respect those whom I come in contact with." "I choose to experience prosperity not only financial prosperity but also be prosperous in my work, my community involvement, and I agree to show my gratitude by being kind and generous with others." "I choose abundance in love, money, joy, health, and gratitude, and I would like to show others the meaning of happiness, and how to be joyful and generous."

FAITH

"So long as we believe in our heart of hearts that our capacity is limited and we grow anxious and unhappy, we are lacking in faith. One who truly trusts in God has no right to be anxious about anything"
~ Paramahansa Yogananda

This prayer will demonstrate that through sustained efforts of holding on to positive thought and action you will achieve what it is you are seeking.

Prayer
I open my mind, heart, and soul to receive faith. I know that with faith all that I desire to be, do, or have is available to me **right now!** When my mind remains open all negative thoughts about myself, my circumstances, and the world around me flows out, and new thoughts, feelings, and ideas of love are able to freely flow in. I realize that the thoughts I allow and hold in my mind will ultimately determine whether I am able to experience my desires. Faith is what makes my journey easier, it strengthens my confidence and increases my conviction and assures me that what I pray for will be made manifest in my life. I know all that is required by the Universal God source is that I truly believe in Its power.

I reject all thoughts of doubt; knowing that my beliefs and faith along with my positive thoughts is all that is needed therefore, I am careful of the thoughts I allow to enter into my consciousness. I have but to choose, have faith, and accept that my prayers have been answered. I thank our Universal God source for giving me the gift of faith which is the key to the lock that holds the answers to all my prayers.

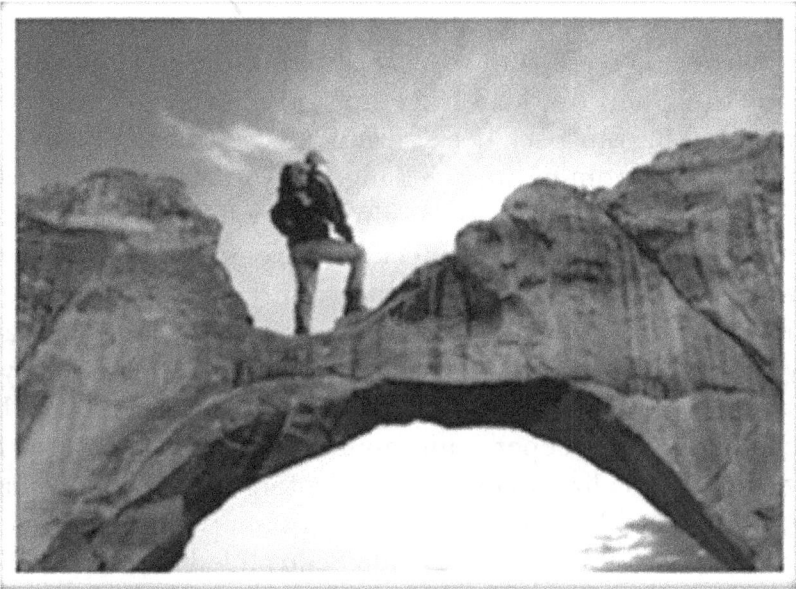

Faith Meditation

As you begin this meditation take the time to make sure you will be uninterrupted, and that you are in a quiet and comfortable environment. Focus on relaxing your body, and mind. Take three deep and cleansing breaths. As you begin envision that you will be taking a journey where you will begin by climbing a steep mountain on a very warm day. Imagine that upon your back you are carrying a very heavy back pack, filled with everything you think will be necessary to sustain you along the journey. Imagine that your pack is filled with everything you may need but you have forgotten your water. You are assured that there will be water but allow your mind to imagine the anxiety you might feel on long journey without water. The more your anxieties grow, the heavier the pack on your back gets. As you become aware of this and realize that your pack is also filled with all your doubts, anxieties, worries, and fears, the weight of it almost becomes unbearable.

As you begin the long walk with this heavy pack you realize that the load is too heavy for the journey in front of you, and your thirst is growing, you must discard something. Your worries continue, your doubt about whether you can actually make the journey increase, and you are afraid of the trek ahead, you decide to lighten you load by getting rid of some of the articles of clothing in your pack because you believe you can make it to the summit without having to change. As you continue, the pack still weighing you down, you begin to pray to find water as you hold onto the things that you feel you have no power to rid yourself of. Your pack is still loaded with your feelings of fear, doubt, worry, and anxiety. Imagine that you continue the long walk, and as you do you are growing more tired and worn. After a while you again feel the weight of the load, it feels even heavier, and the hill ahead has gotten steeper. Your mouth is dry, and as you look for direction you realize that you have also forgotten the map charting your course. Imagine the feelings of disappointment, frustration, and confusion which have now been added to you pack. You are hoping for a natural spring somewhere along the way, but you are uncertain, but you feel assured that there is to be water. Imagine the fatigue you feel knowing that you must continue the journey and lighten your load. Again you must choose what to get rid of. Envision the things remaining that you feel you can rid yourself of is food and medicine. Imagine the doubt you might feel having to make this decision. Both are important, the food is necessary in case you get lost, and the medicine is important in case you get sick. Imagine the feelings of fear that have increased. Allow yourself to experience these feelings, feel their weight and how they make your journey so much more difficult. Although filled with doubt, you believe you can sustain without the food, but imagine the fear, and the weight it bears but imagine that you continue along, praying that at your next stop there will be the water you hope for.

Struggling in the noon day sun, you realize that you have made very little progress. The weight of the pack feels as heavy as it did when you first began. You decide to rest and sit down on a large rock to see what is left in the pack to be thrown away to lighten the load. When you look inside the last article you believe you can get rid of is the first aid kit. Imagine the confusion, and despair you might feel. You cannot imagine why the pack is still so heavy. You cannot see the other things inside such as the growing fear, doubt, frustration, confusion, and despair. You cannot see them, and cannot rid yourself of them, so you continue along, still praying for water.

With your next steps you begin to question yourself, your intentions, your purpose, and ask why this journey is so important. Imagine how confused and doubtful you would be. Imagine all the questions you would have trying to sort out this miserable journey. What made you come anyway? How is it that you forgot one of the most important things you would need, water? What happened to your map, and are you on the right path? How much farther do you have to go, and will you actually make it. Without your knowing it, all these questions of doubt continue to fill the pack you are now carrying. You even begin to question whether to turn back or not but you're more than half way from where you began, and would make no sense to go back so you decide to press on. Imagine the heat, the fatigue in your body and mind. Imagine the weight of this pack that is filled with things you really don't need, and definitely don't want. You realize that in order to be successful at reaching your desired destination you have to get rid of the weight, and believe you can make it. You must shift your load, regroup, and restock. Envision that at your last resting place you finally turn the pack inside out dumping out everything. You care nothing about the first aid kit; you know you won't need it. Also in front of you there lies fear, doubt, worry, frustration, confusion, despair, anger, sadness, thirst, hunger, want, desire, and other feelings you may not recognize. Imagine that also lying before you are feelings of love, faith, gratitude, contentment, confidence, and excitement. You can now see what had weighted you down all along. This time you make a conscious decision to only put the things in you pack that you absolutely need to complete this journey. Imagine that the things you put into your pack are faith because you now know you will be able to reach the summit, you can see it around the bend. You choose confidence because your faith allows you to feel confident about your success. Imagine that you also choose excitement because you are able to feel excited about what's ahead of you. You pick gratitude because you realize that in spite of the hardship you faced on the journey you are grateful that you have survived it, and appreciative of the lessons you've learned. Imagine that the last thing you put in your pack is love because love is what brought you on the journey, and love is what has allowed you to complete it. Although you continue to be thirsty, your faith allows you to believe that you can make it the rest of the way without it, and allows you to believe that you might still find it before the journey ends.

Envision yourself loading your back pack with a new sense of vigor. Imagine that you are tired, worn out, but you have a greater sense of purpose. Imagine that you might even feel a bit more energized. See yourself slinging the pack onto your back, and confidently taking the next steps towards your destination. As you walk the summit gets closer and closer. You realize that although your pack is filled with things, it is almost weightless. You also realize that everything inside is fortifies you and doesn't weight you down. There is nothing negative left in your pack, on your mind, or in your presence. You can see that your prayers will be answered, and you can feel the excitement and anticipate how good you will feel when your journey is complete. Just ahead less than 100ft before reaching the top of the hill you can see the summit where your desires await you. Imagine that just before you arrive there is a small spring running alongside the mountain filled with crystal clear water. Imagine the joy, and relief you would feel. Envision yourself sprinting to the spring and drinking from it. As you drink imagine that you are overcome with all the feelings in your pack, and your pack becomes totally weightless because now all you were carrying is within you.

Remember
Faith is…. evidence of things unseen… never look at the circumstances that surround you but have complete trust in our Universal God. Lack of faith is when you allow negative thoughts such as fear, and doubt compromise your thinking which will prevent you from establishing the full benefits of our connection with our Universal God source.

Affirmations For Faith

- "I believe that I can achieve any goal I set forth today"

- "I know that anything I truly believe I can truly achieve"

- "I remove all doubt and move forward claiming my desires"

- "Faith allows me to take each step with confidence as I know they will lead me to the desires I choose"

Journal Exercise For Faith

"I tell you, whatever you ask for in prayer, believe that you have received it, and it will be yours"
~Mark 11:22-24

Today your exercise will help you learn to increase your faith, and know that what you ask for, so shall you receive.

The First Step in Having Faith
Faith is the unquestioning belief in something which there is no visible proof or evidence. It is a belief or a "knowing" even though our senses tell us something different and there is no proof that our "knowing" has any validity at all.

Become a Rap Star!
Whether or not you are a fan of rap or hip-hop music, there is a great lesson on faith found during an interview of a rap star. This young man spoke about his success and when he was asked about how he was able to preserve with all the obstacles he faced in his life, and with all the nay-sayers telling him otherwise he simply stated that he knew he was going to be successful and rich regardless of what the people in the entertainment business said. He said he would not allow the thought of anything less than success and riches to enter into his mind, as he visualized his goal.

(It is understood that having faith is not just about amassing great material wealth, but this is simply an example of the power of faith having no boundaries, it is about believing without a shadow of a doubt.)

The Journey – Belief without Seeing

Today you will work to develop your faith, and you will use situations or things you are uncertain of. Because faith is indicative of a "knowing" it's important to note that you cannot fake having faith. If you don't believe or you doubt, you don't have faith, and the Universe will bring you situations that require you to use doubt. To move away from doubt and on to hope, and then faith, you must literally let go of whatever the situation is that is causing you to have doubt. You must realize that you are not able to "fix" the situation if it's not working for you on your own. You must believe that the situation can be resolved or brought to you, you must then put it in the hands of our Universal God source. Once you make that decision, you must let it go, and realize that the worries no longer belong to you, and the resolution of that situation is simply not your concern. "WOW", you might say, "can we actually do that or live that way?" Yes, absolutely, you must live this way if you want to increase your faith, and receive what it is you desire.

Give it to the Universe

Start your journal entry with date, day, time and title it "exercise on increasing faith." Begin by thinking about those things in your life you would like to be able to let go of. They could be issues regarding work, family, or friends. These things could be issues you have with feelings such as feeling anxious, angry, or sadness. You may be experiencing financial difficulties and simply want to be rid of the burden. Think about those things you feel you can right now, let go of and not look back on them. Select a problem or circumstance that you are willing to immediately let go of. You may be tired and frustrated from trying to solve it on your own, or you may believe it is beyond your ability to handle. Write them in your journal. Write down what they are, and the problems they are causing you. Also list what it would feel like or mean if you didn't have to be burdened with them. As you write them in your journal allow yourself to surrender them to our Universal God. Tell yourself that you are honestly and literally letting go. With each one, see yourself placing this "thing" or "problem" on the lap of our Universal God source. After you have done so say:

"In order to reach my higher good, I no longer choose to carry these burdens. I know that by placing them in your hands they will be taken care of, and I am free to experience my life fully and joyfully."

Each time you're able to take a concern or worry and lay it on the lap of our Universal God source, you will begin to feel more confident about leaving those concerns there, and being able to walk away.

When you find it easy to leave things in the hands of our Universal God source, begin to make another selection to place there. It is important to also visualize yourself without the burden of these problems. With each problem you leave, make sure you are willing to let go, otherwise you may find yourself trying to "help" or "fix" the problem again. The more you let go, the more your faith will increase, and the more you learn to trust in our Universal God. As your faith increases, your worries will decrease because you have made the decision to "Give it to the Universe." This exercise will help you learn to survey what you are feeling, remove your worries, gain confidence, and trust, and allow yourself to feel the joy of life.

It is important to remember that this exercise is not intended to replace taking care of things that are within your ability to take care of or to get away from doing those things you know you should do, and are able to do. This exercise is meant for those burdens that are literally beyond your ability to manage, and cause you distress when you think on them. It is also important that you believe they will be taken care of. If you have no belief or hold doubt in your mind, they will simply resurface again in one way, shape or form. You must also accept the outcome after you leave your worries behind, knowing that whatever the outcome, it is for your greater good.

Conclusion

The purpose of this exercise is to learn to recognize the things in your life that are beyond your ability to control or manage, and to let go of them knowing that our Universal God will help you take care of them. By doing so, your confidence and faith will increase which will allow you to experience a much more joyful life. You are not intended to be burdened by troubles. Your life is intended to be filled with joy, and happiness. It is when you allow yourself to take on burdens that are truly out of your ability to manage that your life becomes a burden. Let go, and let our Universal God source take care of it.

In your journal record the feelings you had when you were asked to take your worries to our Universal God source. Answer and record the following information and questions:

1. What was the most difficult part of this exercise? Why?
2. What will need to shift in your mind in order to believe you are able to leave your troubles in the lap of the Universe?
3. What will you do to change those feelings?
4. How will you remember to let go of your troubles?
5. Are you willing to get out of the way, and allow the Universe do Its work?
6. How do you think this exercise will help your faith increase?
7. List some of the other areas in your life that would benefit from exercising your faith?
8. How will gaining and exercising faith do for your relationship with our Universal God source?
9. How will gaining and exercising faith help you in other areas of your life?
10. What is the greatest benefit for you to gain more faith?

In your journal also record the answer to the following statements.

- Today I was able to let go of:

- As a result of letting go, I feel more:

- I have fewer worries and greater faith because I have decided to trust in our Universal God source by:

Conclude your journal entry with an entry that extend gratitude for the experience and all that you have learned as a result of this exercise. Also make a declaration to continue to work on increasing your faith, and sustain it now that you are gaining it.

ATTRACTION

"It's really important that you feel good. Because this feeling good is what goes out as a signal into the universe and starts to attract more of itself to you. So the more you can feel good, the more you will attract the things that help you feel good and that will keep bringing you up higher and higher."
~Joe Vitale

This prayer and exercise will help you understand the power of attraction. You will also learn how through the law of attraction, the power of prayer, visualization, and faith, you can truly create the experiences in life you desire.

Prayer
I seek alignment with our Universal God source, which is all love, light, and power. As I continue this journey, I have learned that I have the power within me to choose what it is that I desire to experience. I am learning how the power of attraction is working within my life, and how I attract the experiences in my life based my thoughts, feelings, ideas, and that which I focus my attention on. Today I choose to be clear in my thoughts so that I may begin to deliberately attract to me all that is good and positive. The clearer I am in my thoughts, choices and desires, the more accurate those things will return to me. I focus my energies on the thoughts I think and on the words I speak, and on the images I hold within my mind.

I have the power to cast out into the Universe that which I do not desire and choose to receive back what I do desire, so I choose goodness, I choose happiness, I choose graciousness, I choose peacefulness, I choose prosperity, I choose abundance, and love. These choices I make knowing that I will attract the same. I remain in gratitude for that which I know is already present in the Universe and on its way to me now. I need not hold back in my requests believing that my prayers may somehow deplete our Universal God's bountiful supply for I know that these things are limitless. Our Universal God source is abundant in all things, and shares this abundance with me. I know that all I desire will manifest in my life, and all that I give out returns to me multiplied.

Attraction Meditation

Find a comfortable, quiet place to sit and relax for at least fifteen minutes of uninterrupted time. Take three deep cleansing breaths, relax, and let go of all the thoughts and concerns of the day. Take time to acknowledge the sounds around you, and slowly let those distractions dissipate. As you relax, begin to visualize a light in the center of your forehead. Quiet your mind, knowing that the better you are able to clearly focus on your inner light, the more clarity you will experience.

As the thoughts and sounds around you melt away, envision yourself walking down a path made of smooth polished stones. As you walk down this path noticing the peacefulness, the calm and quiet, allow yourself to enjoy your surroundings. Feel the warmth of the day, and the brightness of the sun. As you look further into your surroundings notice that overhead is a canopy of tall, stately trees, providing shade from the sun, and keeping you cool and comfortable. As you continue this peaceful walk, imagine that at the end of the stone path you find that you are standing at the edge of an orchard, full of manicured trees, vines, and brightly blooming flowers of every imaginable color and shape. Allow yourself to capture the picture of this wonderful sight. Smell the fragrance of the flowers, and see the vividness of the colored flowers growing and hanging from the vines as they wrap themselves around each tree. Envision that upon the vines are also hanging a variety of the most beautiful and succulent fruit, full, ripe, and bursting with juice and goodness.

While standing on the edge of the orchard allow yourself to take in all the beautiful sights around you. Continue to feel the slight warm breeze blowing gently across the field. Envision yourself seeing people quietly sanding at the perimeter of the field, all smiling cheerfully, and inviting you to join them. Just beyond the path lies a beautifully woven basket. As you move towards the trees and people you pick up the basket and begin walking down each aisle picking the perfect and succulent fruit some so ripe their juice trickling down your arms. When you reach the end of the aisle you pass the basket of fruit to the person standing there, and they welcome your gift with a loving smile, and soft touch of their hand as they offer you their empty basket. Again, you make your way down the next aisle, picking the sweet fruit, and after reaching the end of the aisle there stands another person stands waiting, and offering another empty basket in return. You make your way down yet another aisle, reaching for the fruit, picking, and loving the touch, feel, and smell of the luscious fruit and its juices. You again give away the fruit in your basket receiving an even larger one in return. You continue this picking, and giving as you move through the entire orchard never aware of the heat from the sun, or the thirst in your throat. Never do you complain of the ache in your arms and back nor do you acknowledge the labor in this work. You can feel only joy, and an overwhelming amount of love growing each time you hand off the basket to the person willing to accept your gift.

When you have completed the picking, you see that everyone has a basket full of the precious fruit, yet the trees in the orchard are as full as when you first started picking. You take in one last glance of the beauty of the orchard, and of the kind and loving people, and make your way back down the path towards you destination. The closer you get to the beginning, the more refreshed and rejuvenated you become. The nearer you are to the beginning the happier you are. Take a few moments and allow yourself to feel these feelings. Hold their images and feelings in your mind. Fill your heart with the feelings of gratitude this experience left you with. Now that you have reached the beginning of the path imagine that your mind is clear, your body is strong, and your thoughts are pure and loving. You have no memories of hardship; you are fuller than you were when you started. All the goodness you gave away is now within you. You are aware of this goodness, and know that you have received much more of it than you gave away. You have attracted all that you have given away and even more. You are able to leave feeling totally overjoyed.

Remember
The Universe responds to your every thought, ideas, and feelings, so if you speak positively, and think negatively, you cancel out what you truly seek to attain, and bring to yourself the opposite of what you seek. When you are clear in your thoughts, you will produce feelings and ideas of goodness, and you will attract exactly what it is that you put out into the Universe. Work on practicing to keep your focus positive, consciously see yourself where you want to be, with what you desire. Expect that you will receive what it is you desire, and allow yourself to get excited about it, feel those positive feelings and emotions, they have tremendous creative power.

Affirmations on Attraction

- "I cannot be held back from what I truly desire for I attract my desires, and they come to me by way of our Universal God source."

- "My life is full of endless potential. I attract all that I put out to the Universe."

- "I am a being of light, full of creative energy. My thoughts, ideas, beliefs, and feelings attract my experiences; therefore, I am careful and clear in what I think."

- "My thoughts, feelings, and desires are like a magnet, I attract that to me which I choose to experience."

- "The law of attraction is always at work, I must be clear in my thoughts as I will be attracted to those things I cast my thoughts upon."

Journal Exercise for Attraction

As you learn more about the law of attraction you will understand that where you find yourself today, this very moment, you have attracted into your life. You have, in fact, put a great deal of energy into creating the life you are presently living. Even if it is something less desirable than you claim you want to experience. For instance, were you fearful of being in debt, and do you find yourself in debt? Did you worry about your marriage coming apart, and now you find yourself in that situation? Did you concentrate on not getting the promotion at work, and you are now experiencing not having that promotion? These questions could go on and on identifying the different situations that could be currently taking place in your life, and if you thought on it, you would be able to see how your thoughts, behaviors, and beliefs have created exactly what you are now experiencing. Your worry, regret, doubt, and fear have caused more of what you are experiencing than you know. The answer to why, and how you may have created these experiences that you did not want will come a bit later on but simply stated, you have simply been vibrating with emotions, feelings, thoughts, and beliefs that have attracted what you didn't want in your life. Let's take a look at how to begin to change this.

Get Excited!

Every living thing is equipped with a certain level of energy, and this energy creates a certain vibration. As humans we have the ability to alter the amount of energy we produce, and can control the vibration we carry. The control mechanism that allows us to alter our vibration level is called our emotions. Different emotions cause different vibrations, emotions can cause our vibration level to increase or decrease. Ultimately the higher your vibration, the greater your creative ability. Your emotions, whether negative or positive, generate energy. This energy turns our vibration up or down. Our vibration level is how we attract our experiences, again whether these experiences are negative or positive experiences. High positive energy creates a higher vibration level attracting to us more positive experiences. High negative energy creates a higher vibration level attracting to us more negative experiences. Just as these vibration levels can attract positive experiences, they can also attract negative ones as well, that is why it's important to be aware of your thoughts because your thoughts create emotions, and those emotions create experiences.

For this journal exercise we will practice ways to impact our emotions positively, and increase our vibration which will allow those positive experiences to get through. In your journal begin with your normal entry of day, date, time, and journal exercise title. Then, divide your page into two columns and title one column "unwanted circumstances"; label the other "vibration level". You will be listing all those things in your life right now that are unwanted, and you will then assign it a number value of 1 thru 3; 1 meaning significantly less worrisome, 2 meaning moderately worrisome, and 3 meaning extremely worrisome.

(example)

unwanted circumstances	vibration level
unhappy with my job	2
not enough money	3
lack of companionship	2
unable to take a vacation	1

After you have completed this list, take a few minutes to review it to determine whether you have rated the issues currently. Notice whether the negative circumstances with the highest vibration levels are the concerns you have spent the most time and energy worrying about. Ask yourself whether you were actually aware of how much worrying you were doing about this particular thing. Think about whether your negative focus could be contributing to the cause of your distress. This exercise will help you recognize the areas in your life that you need to refocus your attention to and how important it is for you to decrease your worrying, and replace it with a more positive outlook of that situation.

Refocusing your perspective and changing the way you feel about something that you don't like can be difficult, wouldn't you agree? If you don't like something, then you don't like it, and if you don't like it you're not likely to feel good about it. The best way to turn your feelings around about something you don't like is to expose it to gratitude. Look at it with gratitude, and think about what it is in that situation that you can be grateful for. What positive things does it offer you? Even if it offers the slightest benefit of any kind, look for it and offer it gratitude. If you listed that you're unhappy with your job, begin to think about how having this job allows you to pay for some of the things you need in life. If you don't feel you make enough money, and don't like it for that reason, think about how it allows you gain experience in a particular field or exposure to people that you like.

On a separate piece of paper write down what your statements are after you've shown it gratitude. This may be a challenging exercise for many different reasons. You may find it very difficult to list anything positive about something you dislike so much or something that causes you a real problem, but work hard to think about what type of gratitude you can offer it. There isn't one situation that doesn't allow for some level of gratitude, not one. There is something to be grateful for in everything, every situation, and in every person. There are situations, and sometimes relationships that require you look long and hard to find the gratitude in them, but it can be found. You may have to put extra effort in looking, but it's there, it always is.

Gratitude is the sure way of turning those situations or relationships around and rescuing your negative feelings and turning them into something close to positive feelings. This is a very important opportunity and lesson because it offers great practice to learn to use gratitude. This exercise will help you see just how powerful gratitude is, and help you to see the healing benefits of it up close and personal. In fact gratitude is the second most powerful emotion we have next to love. In and of itself, that's exactly what gratitude is, a form of love, and we know that love is the single most powerful force there is. We're not suggesting that you learn to love all circumstances immediately, but we know that the longer you show those things gratitude, the sooner you'll be able to change the way you feel about them, and it is your feelings that will help you increase your vibration level.

Once you have completed the gratitude list, go back and look at the vibration levels you assigned each circumstance. After you introduced and exposed each circumstance to gratitude, determine whether their number should remain the same. Think about whether their levels could have decreased with gratitude or whether they remain the same. In most cases those numbers aren't likely to go up but in many cases they will probably go down. If there is a decrease in their vibration level cross out the original number and enter the new one. Allow yourself to feel the feelings of success; you were able to redirect your emotions towards more positive ones, and that's a huge step in the direction you want to be in to attract positive experiences.

For the second part of this exercise, think about the positive circumstances you are going to attract into your life. Make your intentions clear, and don't be mistaken by thinking you can fool the Universe into manifesting something in your life that you truly don't believe you can have, be or do. Remember, your vibration level will respond in direct relation to your enthusiasm. If you doubt your abilities or the ability that the Universe can or will manifest it, your emotions will reflect that doubt, and that's exactly what you will attract... doubt. If you are uncertain of whether you "deserve" what it is you desire, you will attract circumstances that cause you to feel that you're not deserving of your desires.

After you've made the selections, consider each one individually. Allow yourself to feel the feelings that would come if it were in your life right now, get excite about it, shout for joy, jump in the air, whatever your reactions and emotions would be if it were right in front of you. What would you feel if you received a call that said whatever you desires are was being delivered to you today? What would you feel? What would you do, now be it, do it, act it, become it. You have just received that call, now enjoy it!

In you journal record those things you desire to attract, write about what you learned, and what you need to do to assure that they will be delivered to you. This record is just a reminder of what it is you are able to create, and what you need to do to make sure it arrives. Don't worry about when it will arrive, or how it will arrive, just believe, and know that it will, and remember to keep your vibration up so that it can find its way to you.

ABUNDANCE

"Life is a field of unlimited possibilities."
~Deepak Chopra

This prayer will reveal to you the secret of the ages that if abundance is what you desire you have the ability to attract it into your life today.

Prayer
I am in partnership with our Universal God source who is Omnipotent and ever present in every aspect of my life. I realize that there is an unlimited supply of goodness and love, and that I am deserving of all of it. I know that all my needs can be met I need only to choose what it is that I desire to experience in my life for our Universal God answers all my prayers. I have been provided with all that I need to experience an abundant and happy life, and as I grow closer in my alignment with the Universe It's love and goodness flows freely to me.

Abundance is what I choose to experience, and I am open to the energy which is always been available to me. I remove all thoughts of limitation realizing that that is an artificial barrier as my desires flow freely through the Universe. I believe in the law of attraction, and know that as I give I will receive. I know that I am attracting into my life all that I need abundantly. I trust in the power of the Universe, and thank our Universal God source for all the blessings I will receive.

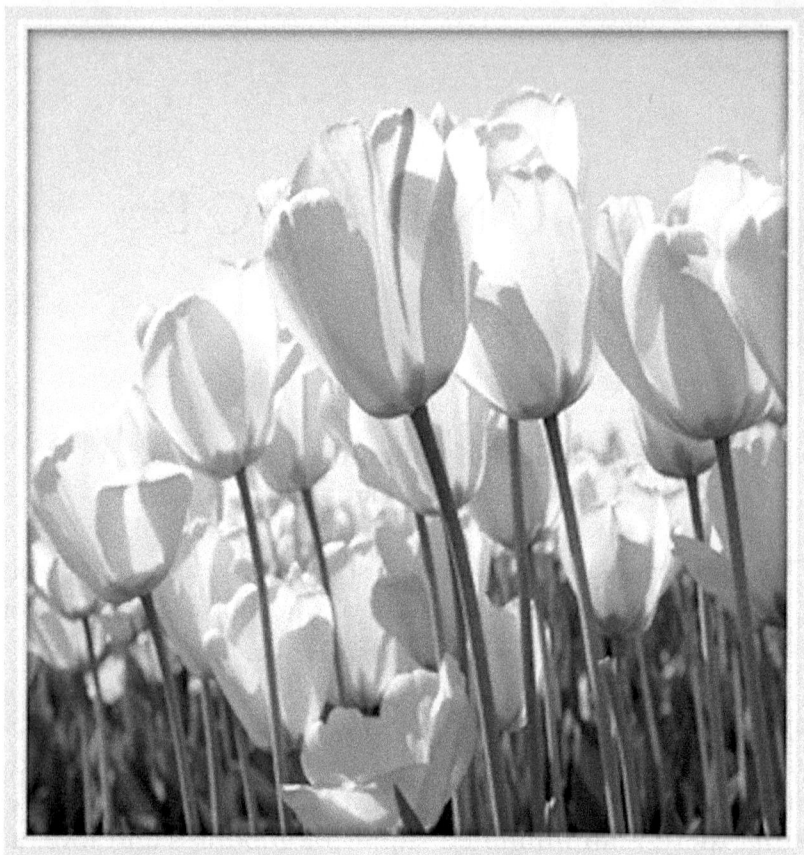

Abundance Meditation

Remember to find a place where you can relax and sit quietly, uninterrupted for 15-20 minutes. Begin your meditation by sitting comfortably, and taking in and releasing a number of deep cleansing breaths.

In this meditation you will not only spend time in silence visualizing yourself as abundant, you will also actively become abundant in your thoughts, and actions. First, quiet your mine, and focus on your own breath. Hear the sound of your own breathing. Are you hearing short and shallow breaths or do you hear long and deep breaths? Work to relax you mind and body and achieve longer and deeper breaths. As you reach this level of breathing, see yourself with abundance, feel yourself as abundant, think of yourself as abundant. Would having a greater salary make you feel abundant? See yourself with it, feel yourself with it, act as if you have it. Would having enough freedom to do all the things you want to do cause you to experience abundance? See yourself doing what it is you would like to do freely. Feel yourself enjoying what you're doing; act as though you can do whatever it is you want to do. Allow those feelings of excitement, joy, contentment, and happiness. Hold them in your mind's eye for as long as you can. Enjoy the feelings of contentment, security, confidence. As you see and feel the excitement of having abundance, pay attention to your breathing. Keep breathing deep, long, smooth breaths. The longer deeper, smoother breaths reflect calm, assurance, conviction, peace, and agreement.

These are all the things you need to "KNOW" the experience of abundance. As you continue to envision yourself abundantly, try to hold those feelings, thoughts, and ideas for as long as possible. Remain there imagining yourself abundantly for as long as you like. Have fun with your images, and feelings. Claim them, make them your own, hold on to them until you are sure of the feelings these images produce. As you begin to come out of the meditation, remember the feeling of "**KNOWING**" you experienced and bring it with you. Now that you are aware of what it feels like to experience abundance keep that "**KNOWING**" with you for the rest of the day. As you go through the day, and if you feel the pang if fear or uncertainty arise go to that "**KNOWING**". Turn on those feelings you brought with you from the meditation. Hold those visions and feelings for as long as you can until you begin to manifest the feeling of abundance all the time. Use those feelings willingly, become comfortable with this exercise, and use it often.

Remember

You are truly abundant but sometimes your life's conditions stand in the way of allowing you to feel abundant at certain times. Also remember that if you are unable to recognize abundance in your current life, how will you be able to recognize it when the Universe brings you more of it? We all have access to the unlimited abundance in the Universe. Get used to allowing yourself to feel this way, expect abundance, and **KNOW IT TO BE SO!**

Affirmations of Abundance

- "I choose to experience abundance in my life"

- "I am able to tune into the unlimited supply of abundance that fills the Universe whenever I choose."

- "I am grateful for the abundance that is currently in my life, and for more that is yet to come."

Journal Exercise For Abundance

"Whatever you are waiting for-peace of mind, contentment, grace, the inner awareness of simple abundance- it will surely come to you but only when you are ready to receive it with an open and grateful heart."
~Sarah Breathnach

Barriers to Abundance

For many people, one of the most difficult virtues to accept as truth is that you can experience abundance and prosperity in your life today. It's difficult to imagine that fact when you feel you have nothing or if you feel that you don't have enough of what you desire. Just as everyone has their own ideas and desires, so to does everyone have their own ideas of what abundance would be for them. Some people believe that abundance is so far away from them that they can't even imagine what the experience would be like if they had it, making it impossible for it to manifest in their life. By developing a healthier, possibly a more reasonable idea of abundance might make it easier to imagine. If this is something you struggle with, consider that abundance is simply having enough of what you want, to do the things you want, when you want.

The main reason for your disbelief is because you may have been programmed to believe that only certain people belonging to certain privileged groups are worthy enough to experience abundance. The second reason is that the idea of seeking abundance seems somehow wrong because our society has convinced you that there isn't enough to go around, and that it isn't polite to expect to have more. The third major barrier to achieving abundance is that you accept these messages, and believe they are true, they are not! You must change the way you think and feel about abundance before you can expect to experience it.

We understand how difficult it is to change the way you think, and how difficult it is to reprogram yourself into believing something that has such deep roots, but that's exactly what you have to do. You not only have to change the way you think about experiencing abundance, you must also change how you view yourself in the world. You must believe that you deserve to not only experience abundance, but you deserve to experience all that you desire. You deserve and are capable of experiencing your greatest dreams and desires; abundance is simply one of them.

It is important to first remember that in order to experience abundance you must be able to recognize it. Abundance exits in your current life, but you haven't been able to pin point where it is. If you cannot recognize where it is currently in your life, how will you recognize it when the Universe brings it to you? If you think and feel you don't deserve or aren't capable of experiencing abundance, even though you would like to experience it, you will not have it. That is not until you change the way you think and feel.

Our Limitless Universe
A major untruth is that there isn't enough to go around. We've been programmed to think there isn't enough food, there isn't enough money, there isn't enough peace, there isn't enough love, and there isn't enough goodness. In truth the only limitations we have are the ones we harbor in our mind. This vast Universe has many secrets within it, but one thing that is not a secret is that it has always sustained life, and will likely continue

to infinitely. It could not be possible for the Universe to produce life, and then not be able to sustain it, and since we are all part of our Universal God source, you can be assured that you will be abundantly provided for. This is a promise from our Universal God source. Whether or not you partake in the abundance is entirely up to you. It is your right to be abundant, and it is a promise that you can be abundant, never doubt it! It has always been your choice, and will continue to be your choice as to what you manifest in your life. It is also your choice to determine what truth is for you, and what it is not.

The truth is that there has always been enough, and always be more than enough to go around.

Exercise 1
In this exercise you will work on changing your thoughts and feelings about abundance, even if only temporarily, in order to create a shift in your perspective. This shift in thinking will help to clear the path of obstacles and barriers that stand in your way of experiencing abundance permanently.

In this exercise you will have the opportunity to visit a very pleasant part of your childhood. Begin by thinking on a time when you were able to be who you wanted to be and literally created your experiences based on your own perceptions and imagination. Think on a time when you didn't know the difference between rich and poor or when you didn't know the difference between more or less. You were probably very young when your perspective was at this level but we're going to tap into that naivety, that innocence, that absolute and unconditional love of life and self. We're going to go back to a time when you were able to pretend and your pretense was true to you. When you were able to crate castles out of sand, and turned mud pies into the most delicious desert. We are going to engage you full imagination where you can use your images, thoughts, ideas, and feelings, to crate exactly what it is you want.

Some of you may find this very difficult since you may have shut yourself off from what is referred to as your "inner child". The world programs to believe that growing up means letting go of our imagination for the most part but our imagination is another one of those gifts from our Universal God source that is here to help us create what we desire. Pretending and make believe have been discouraged after you reach a certain age. It's considered "inappropriate", "immature", "silly", and somehow if done as an adult "misleading" or "dishonest". The total idea of not using your imagination is kind of a contradiction especially since we use it most of the time and are unaware of it. For example, when you're having a really day, and someone asks, "How's your day going?" If you're not comfortable with the individual or don't know the well enough to be honest you **pretend** or **"make believe"** by replying, "oh, not so bad." You may even go all the way and replay, "oh great, how's your day?" You know you're having an awful day but you pretend you're okay anyway. Another example is that when you're in the company of a group of people you may not have much in common with but you want to fit in so you *pretend* and begin acting like them. You may change the way you talk, you may participate in behavior that you wouldn't normally do because you want to be accepted, and not stand out. Can you see the contradiction?

Do you remember how magical it was to make believe? Do you remember being able to create a world so pleasant. Do you remember how clear you vision was, how vivid you were able to see yourself as a doctor or nurse, a veterinarian or race car driver? Make believe truly is magical. In fact if you had an active imagination as a child you may have helped to create what and who you are today. Many people who had a particular passion as a child are now living that passion in their adult lives as a doctor or lawyer, or VP. You imagination is a very essential part of your life. Discouraging the use of it actually disarms you from the use of this powerful gift. Pretending or "make believe" isn't dishonest, it helps you create and enjoy your life the way you want to enjoy it, and isn't that what we're working on trying to do right now? Let's reconnect with your imagination, and remember what it's like to create the world the way you would like. Let's try it together, even if it makes you feel a little silly at first. The more you get into it, the more you'll enjoy it!

Using Your Childlike Imagination

We are going to attempt to recreate a magical experience, one that will help you let go of the ideas that prevent you from experiencing abundance the way you would like. In order for this exercise to be successful, you must allow yourself to let go. You must not worry about how silly it may seem for you to "make believe". As a child, it may have bothered you if others made fun of you, but you didn't let that stop you from pretending because the enjoyment far out weight the enjoyment of it. You went about creating your experience in spite of the teasing. Just like today, the experience will far outweigh any skepticism others may have. Besides, no one need know that you are pretending, unless you choose to share the experience.

You won't be asked to do anything irrational or unreasonable. Simply allow yourself to think and feel deeply enough that your mind is transported into a state of belief. Engage your imagination. The way to do that is to crate thoughts of you experiencing joy. Allow yourself to feel joy, and see yourself experiencing something that would bring you joy. You may be able to hold on to those thoughts for several minutes, and if you really let go, and "go with the flow", these thoughts may last for several hours. The idea is to experience a state of belief long enough to trigger your conscious mind into waking your subconscious into believing the possibilities you are creating for yourself. In your journal write the story of your desires. Write down exactly what you want your life to look like, or feel like. Be as detailed as possible, include your family, the work you would do, the home you would live in, the lifestyle you would lead, the finances you would have. Write about the things you would do in your leisure time. Write it as it you were verbally creating your life experiences. Don't worry about accuracy, and storyline or timeline, those things aren't important. Don't worry about grammar; you can even simply create a list of all these experiences. Feel the joy, and excitement. Get excited about it!

When you have completed your list or story, look it over, feel it, express it through emotions. Feel the butterflies in your stomach from the excitement it creates. Hold those feelings as long as you can. Now, take a step further and close your eyes. Imagine yourself with everything on that list. Imagine you with your family enjoying, the house you will live in, driving the car you want, walking into the building of the perfect job you desire. See yourself sitting behind your desk, in your own office doing the work you love. Imagine that after work you and your friends or family will do something special in your leisure time. What will that be? Will you dine at the restaurant of your dreams, will you shop at your favorite stores. Will you go in the perfect date with the perfect companion? Will you take a trip to a private destination or take the kids to a theme park? What will you do? You create it and then envision yourself doing those things, living that life style. Try to reach that level of enjoyment that almost has you wanting to jump out of your chair and leap into action. Hold those feelings for as long as you can, just let go, and **GO!**

Spend as much time with this as you'd like. Be as creative as you desire, let your imagination take you away. Really make believe, make this experience as believable as possible. After you have spent the time you are comfortable creating this experience into belief, write about how you felt while make believing. Identify the feelings you had, make sure you use as much detail as possible so that when you read on this later you are able to recapture those feelings again. Use this experience as a springboard to creating our next scene, and the next until you have visually experienced each act in your life you would like to create. As you complete the exercise, allow yourself to sit in the joy you have created, and while you do, offer gratitude to our Universal God source for already creating these images and experiences knowing that they are on their way to you right now! Use this exercise as often as you can, there is enormous power in it.

Remember – The Creative Power of Thought
You will experience great creative power in direct proportion to the energy, thought, and feelings you put into this activity. The longer you remain in this elevated state with an elevated vibration, the greater the energy; you are putting into the Universe, and the more you are summonsing and encouraging the Laws of

Attraction to you. When you allow yourself to access this state of mind and awareness, the easier and more enjoyable this exercise becomes because you can really feel what you are creating. You may begin to notice different things coming to you that you had not before. Sometimes unexplained experiences that are in line with experiencing abundance will seem to pop up. Don't dismiss these experiences as coincidences; these are experiences you have helped create with our Universal God source. You can go as far as you'd like with this exercise, as far as you feel comfortable. Some of you may have a very vivid and active imagination naturally, but for others this may take more effort so we offer a second exercise that you may be able to better relate to.

Exercise 2

In this exercise you will build a visual mural which will symbolize the abundance you desire. Begin by gathering all sorts of magazines that you may have lying around the house. You will also need a large poster board, glue sick, and markers. You may also want to gather any type of embellishments such as stickers, post cards, photographs, mementoes that can be glued or tacked onto the poster board. If you have a picture of the exact item or items you want to manifest gather that as well. You may even be able to find a picture of that item in one of the magazines.

To make this mural more meaningful to you, you may want to make an effort to take a picture with whatever it is that might help you experience abundance. For example, if abundance to you represents a specific model of car, take the time to visit that dealership, and take a picture of you sitting in that car. If you're really into this, and you truly desire that particular car try test driving it, if possible, so that you can actually have the feeling of what it would be like to own that car. If you only get as far as taking the picture of you and the car, that's good enough, use it. These pictures produce feelings that are very powerful, and will be added to your mural.

Gather all your items, and at the top of your mural write an affirmation that means something to you; a statement of empowerment that produces images, and feelings that represent the life style of abundance you desire. Flip through the magazines you have gathered, and focus on statements, pictures, words, phrases that will help you crate the picture of this abundant life style. Be select in what you choose, make sure that whatever you choose not only looks like what you want but evoke strong feelings from you when you look at it or read it. You might be led to a picture of a large mobile home traveling down the back roads that matches your ideas of travel. You may be led to a picture of the surf on a tropical island that represents the image of the vacation you want to take with your family. It would be any picture that matches the images in your mind of the things you would surround yourself with, or see yourself doing when you create the experience of abundance.

Begin collecting these pictures, statements, or phrases by cutting them from the magazines. You may select any number of pictures, and crate as many murals as you'd like. Once you have selected the pictures, begin to arrange them on the mural in whatever fashion makes sense to you. Try to create an image that is dynamic and inspirational for you. Allow yourself to feel free to write whatever messages you would like to see when you look at the mural. As you are arranging your mural, take your time and allow yourself to feel the experience of "creation", because that is exactly what you are doing. You are creating you image of a life of abundance. When you select a picture, cast your gaze in such a way that you can actually visualize or imagine yourself in that picture. As you past items onto the mural, continue to create the vision in your mind's eye of you enjoying yourself as you would when you experience abundance. Once the mural is completed pick a special place to hang it. Make sure it is in a place that you will see several times each which will constantly remind your creation of an abundant life.

Now, remember that when you look at this mural you are not looking at it and "*Wanting*" these things but rather you are looking at it as if you are simply waiting for the Universe to bring it into your reality because that is exactly what you are doing. You know these things already exist in the Universe, they already belong to you because you have claimed them, and are casting your emotions and feelings their way to attract them, you expect them to be brought to you. Look at this mural with excitement, and anticipation as if it is expected to arrive any day now. Believe it is possible for you to have these experiences. Know that these are the experiences you will have. Allow yourself to envision the enjoyment of them. Accept the gift of them, they belong to you, you have created this experience. It is important that when you study this mural you keep your mind open to all possibilities for the Universe will move with your every thought in order to create this experience for you. In order to maintain clarity of your creation, try to hold on to the exact same images each time you think of these experiences. Remember that when you are not clear in your vision, you can delay the desired experiences. Notice how things begin to shift and some, if not most of the ideas you created begin to manifest into your reality. This is not magic as your thoughts have creative power, your feelings have power also, and combined they produce creative energy which manifests into reality. Develop a routine where you visit this mural at one point in the day. When you do, allow yourself to feel the experiences that you desire each time you study it.

Conclusion

You are learning about the creative power of thought. Be clear in your thoughts and expect to receive these gifts from our Universal God source. In your journal enter the experiences of abundance you created. Write about the images you created, and how seeing them makes you feel. Also, record in your journal the following information and questions:

1. In the experience today, I was able to create:
2. What did you feel when you experienced abundance?
3. What were you thoughts while creating you mural of abundance?
4. How did this exercise help you?
5. What affect did it have on your life?
6. What did you learn that you will hold onto and use again?
7. Write your gratitude statement for this exercise.

Conclude your journal entry with an entry that extends gratitude for the experience and all that you learned as a result of this lesson.

Also, make a declaration to continue to experience abundance now that you are doing your part to create it in your life.

FEELING WORTHY

"All that we are is the result of our thoughts. The mind is everything, what we think, we become."
~Buddha

This prayer is meant to help rid you of all self doubt, and realize that you are part of our Universal God source making you a precious being worthy of all the goodness in the Universe.

Prayer
This journey has equipped me with many new skills. These skills help me recognize who I really am, and what I am capable of achieving. I know that I am connected to the Universal God source, and no longer doubt my worthiness. I accept that I am worthy of all the blessings I have received from the Universe. I deserve and am worthy of a bountiful life, filled with endless possibilities and potential. This partnership with the Universe has allowed me to realize that all things are possible. I am worthy of all the possibilities. These possibilities allow me to choose to never again question my worthiness. I choose, and deserve to experience prosperity. I choose, and deserve to experience successful relationships. I choose, and deserve to allow myself to be loved unconditionally. I choose, and deserve to allow myself to be successful. I am a precious, loving being, able to receive that which I give, and choose, and deserve to give love so that I may receive it in return.

Feeling Worthy Meditation

Today you will be engaged in an active meditation/exercise. It can be done anywhere at any time. You will work on thinking, and creating powerful thoughts and feelings. Many people have feelings of unworthiness for many different reasons. Many have been programmed to believe that if they've committed some wrong doing in their past that they are attached to that wrong doing forever.

They have been programmed to believe that this deed can never be undone therefore they can never be truly worthy of goodness so they begin to accept, and expect less. They expect, and accept less love. They expect, and accept less recognition, they expect, and accept less goodness, and they accept, and expect to be less worthy. This is untrue. While the wrong doing in your life has consequences, the one consequence you don't have to accept is that you are less worthy or that our Universal God can't or won't love you as others are loved.

There is nothing you can do, no deed that can be committed that could cause anyone to lack worthiness. Feeling worthy isn't something that can be created by someone else, it's a belief you have to have of yourself. It's a state of mind that you have to create, and it is an ongoing process that unfortunately, never stops for some people. We must first work on what changing the feelings of being unworthy. To do this we have to replace your current thoughts of you and your abilities with the truth which is that you are not only worthy, you are remarkable, you are special, you are unique, and you are powerful. Let's see the truth in you. If you are in a quiet place and are able to meditate, please use this as a meditation. When you are out and about completing your daily routine, use the empowerment statements as often as you can throughout the day.

(Mediation): First begin by making sure you are comfortable, and in a quiet environment. Take in and release three cleansing breaths, more if necessary. If you have access to a candle please take the time to bring it into the room with you, and light it. If you don't have one, find a focal point in the room, something bright or shiny. Try to locate something that projects light, it could be something metallic, or could be a lamp. After you've located this item begin to cast you gaze on it. Think deeply on it. Don't focus on what it is and the information you might   receive about it, just focus on the light it projects. As you look into this light imagine that it is a flame flickering with the soft breeze of the air around you. While you're studying this light imagine the power within it. Imagine the strength of the energy within this light. Imagine that with your thoughts you are able to see this light grow brighter, and stronger. Think of yourself as becoming part of the power of this light, and see your own energy begin to merge with the energy of the light. As the two merge the light grows brighter, and the energy becomes stronger. Feel the love of the pure light, and feel the embrace of the power around you, imagine that you are part of the power! Think of yourself, see yourself, and feel yourself becoming strong. As you have these thoughts and feelings tell yourself in front of the light that:

(empowerment statements): "**I am** part of the Universe, and I am strong", go on to say, "**I am** a loving and precious being, deserving of love and goodness". Allow yourself to hear those words, and experience the feelings that go with that statement. Say out loud, **"I am** a unique and special individual, and no one can replace me". Say, aloud, "**I am** not alone on this journey; I have the love of our Universal God source with me every step of the way". Think of these words, and feel the love they offer, know that there is nothing you can do or have ever done that makes you unworthy of the goodness in the Universe. Continue on with the statements of empowerment. Say aloud, "our Universal God loves me unconditionally, and all my wrong doings have forgiven", "**I am** part of the power of the Universe, not my past". Say aloud, "**I am** moving away from all wrong deeds, and onto love, peace, and contentment", "my connection with our Universal God source empowers me and fortifies me", "I have a new outlook and all that no longer serves me has been left behind".

Any other empowerment statements you wish to add to this list, please feel free to do so. Talk out loud to yourself (when you can) so you can hear yourself saying all these positive things about yourself. You are the only one who can convenience you of your worthiness. No one has the ability to make you feel unworthy unless you allow them to, or believe their thoughts over you own. You possess the power to recreate yourself; you also possess the power to destroy the thoughts of unworthiness.

Throughout you day repeat these empowerment statements over again out loud when you can, and to yourself when you have to. It is so important for you to let go of your past. You cannot drag it along on this journey and be successful. You are recreating your life, and there is no place for negative experiences of the past. This is your new beginning, take advantage of it.

Whatever thoughts, and actions you participate in today, remember to make yourself powerful. Feel the power, be the power. If you don't feel power from one thought, have another, and another, and another, each time, allow yourself to move closer to the realization that you are powerful, and worthy. As you move from thoughts, to energy, to power, see and feel yourself becoming filled with light more and more light. Imagine yourself becoming brighter and brighter as power rushes to you. As you become filled with light, and power, your vibration level will increase, bringing you closer and closer to the power source which is our Universal God source. When you are filled with this much light, and your vibration is high, you cannot question whether you are worthy because you are **BEING** worthy! You will have elevated your state of being in such a way that at the moment your vibration level increases, there is nothing that you are not. When you choose to feel worthy, you must **BE** worthy, which is what you already are, you simply have to believe it, and know it.

Remember
Some of you may find this meditation/exercise very difficult, requiring a lot of energy and thought. If this is the case, you are probably starting off from a very low vibration point. That's okay, make a note of that, and remind yourself that you need, deserve, and are worthy to have more happiness, love, and joy in your life, then go back to the empowerment statements and begin to fill yourself up with them. You next step is to then do what it is that is joyful, more often. Do what it is that makes you happy, more often. Express more love, more often. Know that everyone reaches a low point in their life, but not many people care to remain there for very long as we naturally know to do something to change that. Allow yourself these times of low energy, but don't remain there long. The longer you are without joy, the longer you are without energy, the longer you are with energy, the lower your vibration level;, and the lower your vibration level, the farther you are from reaching the power source, our Universal God. It takes effort to remain connected but if you can, remember to make time to reenergize yourself each day or even several times each day. It will be easier to remain connected, and the more connected you are, the more you can just **BE!**

Affirmations On Feeling Worthy

- "I am capable of achieving greatness!"

- "I possess great intelligence, great potential, and great power."

- "I am worthy of all the goodness in the Universe."

- "I need never ask for worthiness for I am never without it."

- "I am not my past; it doesn't serve who I am today."

- "I am worthy of the unconditional love of our Universal God source."

Journal Exercise On Feeling Worthy

"Sometimes we deny being worthy of praise, hoping to generate an argument we would be pleased to lose."
~Cullen Hightower

On this day, you have selected to work on changing your inner thoughts and beliefs about a most special topic, YOU. In this world of materialism and competition, people have created illusions that literally hide who they really are. People have become conditioned to believe untruths, and use external factors to measure who they think they are, and who others perceive them to be. From the time you were a child, you were measured by someone else's idea of what they thought you should be. These ideas followed you throughout your life. Because you were so impressionable at such a young age, you were given very little, if any choice but to believe, and accept what others' told you about yourself. You were told that you "couldn't do this because you weren't good enough", "don't' try that because it's not for you". The words "can't" and "don't" were some of the first words you learned aside from "no". What you likely learned from these statements is that "you weren't good enough" for this or that. This is a very powerful statement, and if you are a parent, you are probably just as guilty as all the other 300,000,000 parents are in our society. Although no harm was meant, unfortunately, you carried these thoughts, and ideas about yourself all of you life on some level. You probably believed your parents, they are your parents for goodness sake! You not only learned to use these statements and value to define yourself, they helped you learn to define others, and the world around you as well. We grew up believing that if it "can't", it's not good, and if it's not good, it's not worth anything.

This practice has caused you to become very critical of yourself, and the world around you, which has made it difficult to see the real good in the world. It definitely caused you to struggle to see the real good in others. You are further conditioned to believe that you can overcome the idea of not being worth anything by accumulating what is believed to be things of value, "material possessions". You begin to use these "possessions" to determine your worth or value as well as the value of others. You continued the cycle of thinking, and probably tell yourself that if you don't have certain "possessions", you are not good enough. All of these messages of unworthiness, whether you are saying or thinking, "if I don't look a certain way, there's something wrong with me", or "if I don't think or act a particular way I won't fit in" are unhealthy and can cause you to feel unworthy. These thoughts are poison. They distort your values, and destroy your ideas, and cause you to forget who you really are. They cause so much internal pollution that you are almost forced o look externally for ways to define yourself because it's too painful to look at the internal image you have of yourself. What makes changing this situation so difficult is that you believe what you have been told about yourself, and this belief system has very deep roots within you. How then can you be expected to have any positive thoughts of yourself or of your situation, especially if you happen to fall short of the "public's" idea of "normal" or "good" or "cool"? You can't have many positive thoughts of yourself as long as you continue to believe that you are not worth anything, and if you continue to use someone else's value system to judge yourself by. The most important question you should ask yourself is, "how does it make sense that I am part of our Universal God source but also not worthy of the goodness in the Universe?" How can this be true? It cannot be true, and it is not true!

Now that you have a better understanding of how and why you may have formed some of the negative thoughts you have of yourself, maybe you can spend a little time changing them. We can start with you doubts of the idea you have chosen to hold on to. As long as you doubt the information, there is no room for change. If you didn't have doubt, you wouldn't be here at this exact moment, studying about how to change your life. So, let's begin to create new and more accurate information about you. You are a divine being, made in the image of our Universal God. You are a being of light, and love. You are connected with everything in this world, and you are the co-creator of your own life. You have a direct link and personal connection with the most powerful entity in the Universe. You possess the ability to create and experience life as you would have it, and you do not need anyone's permission to do so. It is an inherent gift from our Universal God, meaning that you inherited these gifts, and abilities from our Universal God, they belong to you. You are whatever you choose to be, and are able to create whatever you want to experience. If you can only believe one of these truths about yourself, you are on the right path. So let's continue the journey of discovery. You are going to recreate yourself as a worthy individual with all the abilities, gifts, and talents you choose to have in your life. The way you begin is to start a list of all the things that you are not.

In your journal make the normal entry of date, day, time, and journal exercise. Begin by making a list and call it, "What I used to think of myself". On this list should be all the negative thoughts and beliefs you had of yourself. For instance, you might write: "I used to think I was negative, angry, and unkind. I feel unloved, unworthy, and don't feel like I have much of a future. I don't know how to show love to others because I'm afraid I may get hurt. I feel weak and afraid all the time, and don't have any courage." Make sure you list all the things you used to think of yourself. Try not to leave anything out, no matter how painful it may be to bring the thought up. Don't worry; you are going to get rid of all those painful thoughts and ideas.

On a different page, begin a list and call it, "All the things that I Am". This list should be all the things you desire to become. All of the statements you make must begin with the two most powerful words in the Universe, **I AM**. It might begin like this: "**I AM** loving and lovable", "**I AM** kind, and deserve kindness", "**I AM** worthy, and deserve all the goodness in the Universe". You might go onto say,

"**I AM** a positive person, and try to treat others well", "**I AM** honest and trustworthy". Take your time to write down all the positive things you are now, and desire to become. Do not leave anything out, think deeply and list everything. Once you have completed the list, read it over slowly. Allow yourself to hear the statements, to feel them, and to become them. Read this list over and over again, many times, even after you feel yourself becoming these wonderful things, continue to use this list. Add to it if you can think of anything else. Make sure that you continue to do the things that would reflect all the things you want to create, and those things you envision yourself as. The list of "what I used to think of myself" can go straight into the trash. You can throw all those things away right now because you have made a different choice about your feelings. You have changed your mind about how you define yourself. You no longer want to define yourself by your old descriptions, and they no longer suit you. The list no longer serves any purpose, so get rid of it, and remember, also get rid of those old thoughts you might still be carrying around inside your head.

Conclusion

This exercise should uplift you. You have given yourself permission to let go of the old thoughts, feelings, and ideas that kept you feeling unworthy and unable to experience life as you would have it. You have given yourself the ability to recreate our life anew. You have allowed yourself to move beyond the images that held you captive, so celebrate! Spend time with this list allowing yourself to feel who you really are. Remember that your thoughts and feelings posses creative power, you can literally be transformed from the old you to the new you by simply believing, and now being that new person. Believe these things that have always been true about you, it will enable you to create your worthiness, and whatever wonderful life you choose.

In your journal record the following information, and answer the following information.

1. What was it like to list the old thoughts you had of yourself?
2. What allowed you to let go of those old thoughts?
3. How do you feel about your new thoughts, and beliefs of yourself?
4. How will these new thoughts and feelings affect your life?
5. What would you like to experience now that you realize that you are worthy?
6. How do you think your life will change as a result of changing your thoughts?
7. How will you go forward from here on with you new ideas thoughts and beliefs?

Conclude your journal entry with a statement that declares your worthiness, and record all that you learned as a result of it. Also make a declaration to continue allowing yourself to feel worthy now that you have gained it.

SELF-REALIZATION

"What you are is much greater than anything or anyone else you have ever yearned for. God is manifest in you in a way that He is not manifest in any other human being. Your face is unlike anyone else's, your soul is unlike anyone else's, you are a significant individual, and unique unto yourself; for within your soul lies the greatest treasures of all ~ God."
~Paramahansa Yogananda

This prayer will remind you that as you continue your journey through life, you will continue to gain more and more wisdom, and understanding of your direct experience with our Universal God – that is Self-Realization.

Prayer
I realize that I am a divine being, "having a human experience". During this human experience I have been conditioned to have beliefs about myself that are not true. I realize that any negative thoughts I have about the way I look is untrue. I realize that any negative thoughts I have about not being worthy is untrue, all negative thoughts about me are untrue. I now realize that many of the negative thoughts I had about myself were not true. I know that **I AM** a part of the Universal God source, therefore, **I AM** all things. I also know that in being part of the Universe I have the power to choose who **I Am**, and what I desire to experience. Therefore, through the declaration of **I AM**, I claim all that is

good for **I AM** strength, **I AM** joy, **I AM** capable, **I AM** intelligent, **I AM** deserving, **I AM** One with the Universal God source.

Affirmations

- "**I am** made in the image of God, and realize that **I am** eternally connected to the source."

- "**I am** all things in the Universe, and all I see is a part of me."

- "**I am** connected to the power in the Universe, therefore I possess power."

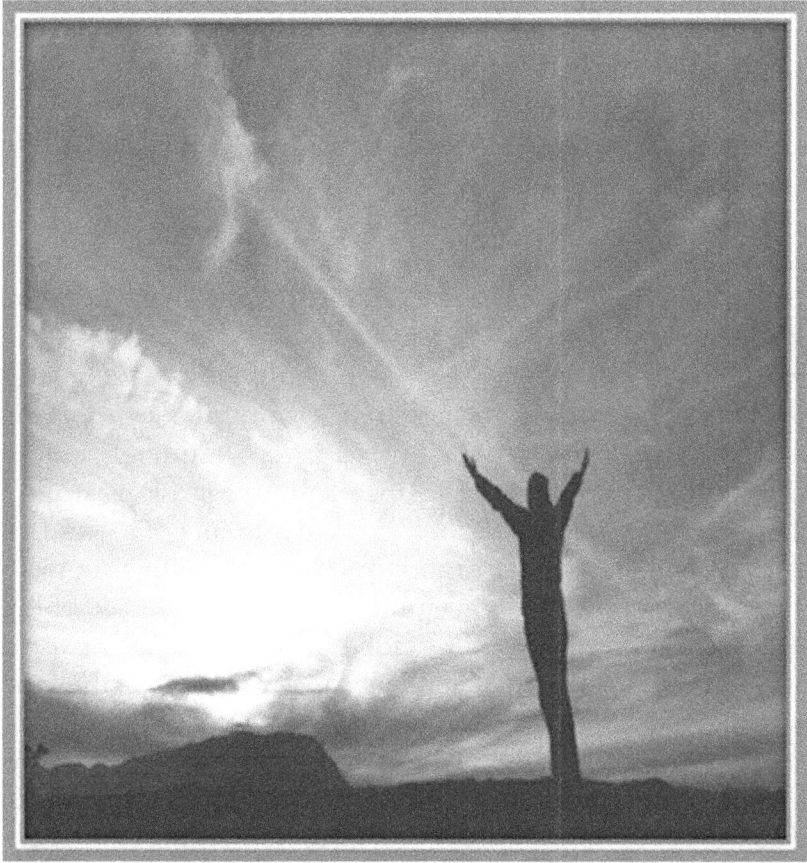

Self-realization Meditation

For this meditation, take the time to find just the right space to receive and experience peace, beauty, and unconditional love. Find a spot in your most favorite room of the house, or you can go to our most favorite place outdoors, maybe to a park or go on a nature walk. This meditation is wonderful for any place that brings you joy. Make yourself comfortable and feel the joy thus place brings you. Envision yourself being wrapped in feelings of joy; stay there with those feelings of joy, and love, and beauty for as long as you like.

Close your eyes, and allow yourself to hear the sounds around you. Whatever they are, feel them, enjoy the sounds, and now wrap yourself in these sounds that are love. Take a deep breath, and hold it a second, then slowly blow it out through you nose. Do this again. Take a deep breath, hold it, and slowly release it through your nose. Take the last breath in, and as you do, make a note in your mind of the scents you smell. Focus on the fragrances you love, whether it is a fragranced candle burning in the room or the smell of some incense slowly burning, or the fresh smell of the outdoors. Take in these smells and imagine being wrapped in a cocoon with the feelings of love, joy, beauty, confidence, and security. Let those feelings saturate you soul. Allow yourself to feel how each of these things can help change your life. Imagine yourself changing, within this cocoon; feeling, smiling, happy, full of curiosity, and love, completely enjoying the embrace. Hold that image n your mind for a long while. As old thoughts try to enter our mind, excuse them gently, and refocus on that image of you wrapped so lovingly. Allow yourself to excuse any thought that pops up trying to recognize the old you. Kindly excuse them and then refocus again. The longer you are able to hold this thought of yourself surrounded by all these positive and loving things, the longer this experience will last.

When you are ready, slowly open your eyes, keeping your mind on your experience. Stay focused on the love you felt within the cocoon. Before you go on, take a deep breath, remembering what it felt like to feel love unconditionally. Also remember what it felt like to be tucked within your cocoon full of love, beauty, joy, and peace. Now imagine yourself beginning to emerge from within the cocoon you had been tucked away in. As you begin to shed the cocoon, you see yourself emerge with the new image of love, peace, joy, and beauty. You have come through this metamorphosis as a beautiful butterfly, and have left the caterpillar behind. You now have the right information about yourself in order to now take flight. You know the truth, you have the confidence, you possess the wisdom, and you recognize the unconditional love that surrounds you. Now you can fly.

Remember
Whenever you want to change the way you imagine yourself, use this meditation. Imagine yourself as a caterpillar, choosing

to experience yourself as a butterfly. Go through the process of being inside the cocoon but take with you all the things you would have yourself be, and when you emerge, bring with you those things that you have chosen. When old thoughts of who you were attempt to creep in, simply excuse them, for they have mistaken you for who you were, and don't recognize you for who you are. The old useless thoughts cannot recognize you as who you really are.

Journal Exercise For Self- Realization
This may be a difficult exercise for many of you because we are going to ask you to create an idea of a relationship you would like to establish with our Universal God source. You may have been taught that the only type of relationship you can have with God is one of subservience. Entertaining the idea of being in equal partnership with our Universal God source may be too much to fathom but remember, you are made in His image. You are One with the Universe, and it is your relationship with our Universal God source that will allow you to be successful at creating your life as you would have it.

If it is that you believe you have the power and control to make your own choices, and if you believe that there is nothing you needv do to be deserving of God's goodness, you must also believe that your ability to choose and have free will allows for a certain amount of power and control. You must possess the ability to voice your desires in order for them to be answered. Clearly you can see the correlation between your role and the role the Universe plays in this relationship. You are encouraged to make choices. You are encouraged to utilize the powers and gifts that have been given to you. You must be able to determine in your own mind the type of relationship you would choose. Let's journey a bit further and begin to create the type of relationship you would choose to have with our Universal God source. Let's think about what thoughts and feelings need to be in pace to allow you to feel empowered in this relationship.

Begin by first recording in your journal the day, date, and time. Also include the title of the journal exercise.

First, describe exactly what it is you're looking for in this relationship. For example:

"In this relationship between me and our Universal God source, I would like to experience companionship. I would like to feel that I can depend on the Universe when I am feeling lonely to provide me with comfort. I would also like...

Answer the following questions, and record this information in your journal. This information will help you compose your agreement. Ask yourself:

- What kinds of things would be present in the relationship?

- What type of evidence would need to be present?

- What are you willing to do to maintain this relationship and connection?

- How important is this relationship to you?

- How will you use this relationship to benefit you?

- How would this relationship make you feel?

- How will you resolve problems in this relationship?

- What are some of the things you would like to share in this relationship?

While these questions may appear difficult to answer, they really are very much like the kinds of things you would expect to find in any loving relationship. Establish where trust would fit into the relationship. How would you display your trust, and how would you know you can trust in the relationship. Obviously, our Universal God source completely understands what is required in a successful relationship. But you would be surprised to find out that there are many individual who don't really know what to expect from any relationship. This exercise gives everyone the opportunity to define what a relationship is, and to discover the necessary ingredients to make a relationship work.

No relationship is one sided, it requires give and take. There is something that both partners must offer in order for it to work. What do you have to offer our Universal God source? Remember your worship and praise is nice but not necessary. What's necessary is your appreciation, your gratitude, your honesty, your attention, your focus, and dedication. Just in case you needed a few pointers, I've provided you with a few helpful hints to help you move along.

Remember, this is your relationship, and if you are to be successful you must be able to see yourself working hand and hand with our Universal God source co creating your desires. This exercise is intended to work as a guide for you to use to be aware of the importance of this relationship, and for you to understand your role in it. It also helps you understand how all relationships work, and hopefully will inspire you to begin to take a look at the relationships in your own life, and discover whether the necessary ingredients are present for them to be successful. If they are not, you will have an idea about how to correct them. You may learn about what is missing from some of your more important relationships, and begin to work on creating them so that they serve your higher good, as well as the good of the other individual involved.

We realize that this is a very unique concept, and one that be extremely difficult for many of you to accept. It may take time, and many of you may have to allow this process to occur on its own time. No matter what your choice is about the type of partnership you have with our Universal God source, we only wish you the very best of luck with creating a relationship that allows you to experience your full and complete greatness. Don't forget that establishing this relationship may reflect some of the other relationships you have as well. Allow your true self to shine through, and be you!

In your journal record and describe the type of relationship you are choosing. Write about what things you bring to the table, and what you hope to gain from this most precious relationship. Also record a statement of gratitude so that you get in the habit of offering your gratitude and appreciation in every relationship you're in.

PEACE

"But peace does not rest in the charters and convents alone.
It lies in the hearts and minds of all people. So let us not rest
all our hopes on parchment and on paper, let us strive to build
peace, a desire for peace, a willingness to work for peace in the
hearts and minds of all of our people. I believe that we can.
I believe the problems of human destiny are not beyond the
reach of human beings."
~John F. Kennedy

This prayer will reveal to us that we are all equally responsible
for bringing peace upon the earth and through our prayers
we can bring about change.

Prayer
I accept my newly found realization of being One with our
Universal God source. In accepting this truth I realize that
the love I am blessed to receive from the Universe is not limited to me, it flows abundantly and unconditionally to every
soul in our Universe. I know that in the mind of our Universal
God source there is no separation between me and my fellowman because we are all One. It is through our connection with
our Universal God source that enables unconditional love to
flow from the Universe to me, and from me to my fellowman.
There is power in our ability to love unconditionally as love is
the strongest force in the Universe. Love can end all wars, it
can heal all wounds, and it can create everlasting peace and

harmony. I choose to be a vessel filled with unconditional love, and I choose to spread peace wherever I go. I strive to be harmonious with those around me, and I know the only way this can be achieved is by loving unconditionally. When I look into the faces of my fellowman I cannot see race, religion, culture, or any other artificial barriers because there is no separation between us. When I look into their faces I must only see myself, and the love of our Universal God source for in the face of love is where I shall find peace.

I pray for peace, asking that my prayers be joined with the countless other prayers for peace that resonate continuously around the world. I know that together we can call on the power of the Universe, and through our prayers e can help bring about change, and learn to embrace peace.

Peace Meditation
As with all the other meditations, prepare by making yourself comfortable. Take the three deep, cleansing breaths. Allow yourself a few extra minutes to quiet your mind and relax. Close your eyes and envision yourself taking a sea voyage. Imagine that this is your first trip out to sea, and you are feeling a little uncomfortable, not fearful but just a little uncertain. After you have boarded the ship, you are warned that there is a storm approaching, and you see the once clear blue sky begin to turn grey as the clouds begin to swell and gather thickly in the sky. Just within a few minutes the once grey sky begins to turn dark blue, and black. The clouds have gone from seeming irritated, to being enraged, full of threat and danger. The sound and force of the wind is deafening, and you cringe as fear begins to sweep onto the ship.

Imagine that as the ship rocks back and forth, and as it does you are able to hear the fearful voices and cries for help from other passengers who have also become fearful of the storm. Take a moment and think on the feelings you have, the feelings of uncertainty, fear, and anxiousness. In your mind you are able to envision every frightening vision you can imagine as your heart ponds against your chest and your breathing increases rapidly. You believe that there is no way to escape what is inevitable, yet you don't want to think about it either. Imagine that you begin to work at regaining some control by telling yourself that you're going to be alright. While you continue to regain your senses you notice that somewhere in the distant you are able to hear the faint sound of melancholy voices chanting in unison. At first you cannot make out what the voices are saying, as the words are intelligible. Imagine the feelings you might have. You notice that the calmer you get, the more distinct the voices become, soon you are able to hear the words of the chant, and they are "peace, peace, peace." It is as if the voices are rolling in on the waves as they crash against the side of the ship. Imagine that you hear the word, "peace, peace, peace" being repeated over and over again, softly but firmly, "peace, peace, peace". Envision that as the chants grow clearer the waves grow calmer, "peace, peace, peace." Imagine that now the clouds began to break as streams of sunlight make their way through the lifting clouds. Now the clearer the skies become, the quieter the chants, they have dropped to the sound of whispers, "peace, peace, peace". The sea becomes calm, and the clouds move away, revealing the brightness of the sun and sky again. The chanting has peacefully faded completely away as the sky is now blue and the sun burning bright and clear.

Sit for a few minutes as you bask in the sweetness of the peace surrounding you. Realize that you can help create the peace that you now feel. Your decision, and attempt to regain control created the joyous peacefulness you are now experiencing, relax, and enjoy it.

Remember

You have the power to make a difference when you are aligned with the power of the Universe Consider the, if you combine your prayer with the prayers of others the world can be changed for the better, and peace could spread like wildfire.

Affirmations For Peace

- "In this moment I embrace peace, and reject fear."

- "I live and enjoy a peaceful life."

- "I open my heart to accept the peace of our Universal God's unconditional love."

- "I choose to be an ambassador for peace and unconditional love."

Journal Exercise For Peace
"Peace I leave with you; my peace I give you. I do not give to you as the world gives. Do not let your hearts be troubled and do not be afraid."
~John 14:27

What better time to address the subject of peace than today. The call for peace has been made time and time again. Can we bring peace into our lives and can we assist in bringing peace upon the earth? The answer is "yes" to both questions. A sage once said, "We need not rush bringing about our desired goals because we have until eternity to accomplish them." But, ask yourself, do you truly want to wait an eternity to help bring about peace across the globe? Do you really want to wait an eternity to achieve peace in your life? We have all heard the arguments, and perhaps we have seen said to ourselves that we as individuals feel powerless to do anything to actually bring about the peace the world needs. Many people have become callous to the concept of world peace, and even poke fun at those who dares to utter their desires of achieving peace in the world. These feelings of powerlessness are often discouraging and downright frustrating for those who would willingly campaign from one side of the globe to the other to be given a small glimmer of hope at achieving world peace. These individuals deserve praise for their efforts and dedication but what many of them don't know is that they are missing the key ingredient to achieving world peace, and that is to first work on achieving peace in their own reality before they can expect to manifest it in the reality of others.

World peace is more than a "concept", it is actually achievable but we're all in such a hurry for it to occur that we have over-looked that simple key. It has to be achieved in each and every one of our own reality before it can be created in the lives of oth-ers. The irony in that statement and belief is that once we create peace in our own individual lives, the world would be at peace, wouldn't it? Let's begin this peaceful journey, and focus on what truly makes all the difference in the world, creating peace in our own lives.

In this exercise you will work on becoming consciously aware of how to create peace in your own life, and also understand your contribution, and God-given power to help move the world closer to achieving Peace. Everyone who has ever been inter-ested in how peace is established and agreed upon by opposing forces is aware of the tool that is used. That tool is called a "Peace Treaty". This tool has been used throughout history, and while it hasn't always been effective, it is a strong tool which can be uti-lized to assure that all the issues important to those involved are recognized, acknowledged, and included. We will use the idea of creating a "Peace Treaty" as part of our exercise as well as utiliz-ing the power of prayer by helping you write your own prayer for peace.

Peace Treaty
There are many different parts of an official peace treaty but for the purposes we need, and for the sake of this exercise it is presented in the most simplistic form. Also, remember, this is your peace treaty between you and the Universe, and can be very informal or as official and as detailed as you choose for it to be.

The exercise is intended to be fun, creative, and inspiring, enjoy it. You can choose to invest as much time into it as you choose or it can be short, simple, and efficiently direct. However, please don't rush. Make this a meaningful experience, be focused about what it is you are working to achieve, and be consciously aware of the energy you're projecting. Your energy affects your vibration level which has creative power.

The things that are important to address in the treaty are specifically the areas in your life that you feel need more peace. Next, it will be important to:

1. Decide how those areas will be addressed. Will you use your journal to express the feelings? If the areas involve other individuals, will you speak to them directly, will you write them a letter or send them an email, or will you call them on the phone to address the issues?
2. Define the prohibitive behavior in other words, set boundaries for how you will conduct yourself, and how you will allow others to conduct themselves when you are addressing these issues.
3. Decide what the expected outcome will be. Ask yourself what you will do to assure the agreement reached will continue. If you are working on eliminating stress in your life to gain more peace, what will you do to eliminate stress and maintain a stress free lifestyle?

Begin by identifying the areas by stating, "these are the areas that keep me from acquiring peace in my life or from feeling peaceful."

*   Family conflict

*   Conflict on the job

*   Financial turmoil

*   Health issues

- Relationship problems

- Lack of spiritual growth and development

(example)
Family conflict – I choose to create peace within my family. In order to establish peace these are the things that I must do to assure that it occurs.

1. I must be willing to address the problems that are creating problems.
2. As a family we must begin to communicate with one another respectfully, honestly, and without hostility.
3. We must acknowledge, and respect the feelings and needs of others.
4. We must agree upon a solution that allows the needs of the family to be met, and work towards achieving the greater good of our entire family.
5. Identify the needs of each family member and work together to make sure that those needs are met by working within the means of our family.
6. Openly express problems and concerns and voice them in the form of constructive criticism, and not complaint's or put downs.
7. Make sure that when problems or concerns are expressed that they are heard and validated.
8. Create time to spend together as a family.
9. Be able to identify the things we appreciate about each family member, and make sure they are expressed.

As you list each area, also write down the things that need to occur to make sure peace can be established and maintained in your life. These are simply examples of how you might make sure that everything within each area is addressed.

(example)
Conflict on the job.

1. Identify the problem.
2. Determine what my contribution to the problem is, and provide a solution to change it.
3. Acknowledge the feelings and concerns.
4. Develop a solution that would minimize the problem.
5. Follow the appropriate channels to address the issue.
6. When there are others involved, especially in a work environment try to resolve the problem directly with the individual rather than get other coworkers involved, if possible.
7. If there is a need for outside involvement, try to work with an individual who can be non-biased, possibly a supervisor or manager.
8. Be honest, and open to hearing criticism, offer constructive criticism, and accept responsibility for your contribution to the problem.
9. Most importantly, remember the purpose is to create more peace, and in order to do that you must reflect love. Your entire approach to any problem must first come from a loving heart, and the end result must be one that will generate more love, and then peace will follow.

(Each work environment may have a specific protocol to follow when addressing conflict. Make sure you are following that protocol first. These examples are simply ideas to use while creating a resolution to the problem).

Once the areas have been addressed, the steps to take to resolve the issues have been taken, and an agreement with all involved has been reached, it would be helpful to create an actual agreement, or "treaty" that reflect the exact exercise. List the issues, resolutions, and agreements. While it isn't necessary to officiate the "treaty" by having it signed by all parties, etc. It may be important for you to have what looks like an official document which may symbolize the importance it has for you. Under certain circumstances it might be extremely helpful for you to use this type of document when addressing family issues or issues within relationships. Some families use these "treaties" as contracts or as formal agreements. It truly is up to you to structure it the way that best suits your needs. The point it makes for this exercise is more symbolic in meaning, although it surely could be used otherwise.

The important fact to remember is that these exercises are intended to inspire your imagination, and help generate creative thought. They are also intended to create visual images that will allow you to use each exercise as a tool to deepen your experience on a particular prayer topic. It's important that you use these tools in a way that will allow you to relate to it and to the experience enough to begin to create that which you desire. Let's move onto creating a prayer for peace.

When you begin to create the prayer again, remember that there is no formal way it must be done. You can create your prayer to reflect the things in life that are important to you. Each one of us has our own idea of what peace means, and of what peace looks like for us, and that's okay. What is important to remember is that love is the only thing that can create peace so your prayer should be filled with ideas, thoughts, and feelings about love which will ultimately bring about peace.

In your journal begin your prayer for peace, and allow your feelings of love to flow. Cast love onto all the areas you feel need peace, in your life, in your neighbor's life, in your church, on our planet, in our world. It is truly up to you to design you own lovely prayer for peace. The next step is to use it!

Conclusion

Remember that you are making a contribution to how this scenario of peace and living life on earth happens, whether your thoughts and feelings are negative and judgmental at any given point, or positive and loving. All is sent out into the Universe, and it responds accordingly. We must all do our best to create the love in our lives and on this planet so that peace can exist, for it is only when we can look on each other with unconditional love that we will experience true peace.

LOVE

"We cannot live only for ourselves. A thousand fibers connect us with our fellow men, and among those fibers as sympathetic threads, our actions run as causes, and they come back to us as effect."
~Herman Melville

This prayer will help you awaken and reconnect with the concept of love on a Universal level.

Prayer
I acknowledge the greatness of the Universal Power, which is God, and know that our Universal God source is love, Love creates and unifies us all and I accept this wonderful gift of God's love. I am thankful that I am connected to and I am a part of our Universal God source. I realize that the connection is not limited in any manner. I feel love radiating through me, and surrounding me. God's love is unconditional, requiring nothing o me to be or do in order to receive it, and it unifies us all as One.

I know that the love I send to another, I also send to myself, and every negative feeling or thought will be sent out to circle the Universe and return, bringing those negative thoughts and feelings right back to me. With this knowledge, I will stand guardian over my works and thoughts, as they have creative power. Whatever good I want to experience for myself, I also want others to experience in their lives. The love of our Universal God source cannot be held back from me, and I am the only obstacle in the way of experiencing that unconditional love. Ever unloving act that diminishes one of us diminishes us all. I reject all negativity, and open my heart, soul, and mind to the love.

Affirmations For Love

- "Universal God is love."

- "The love of the Universe encircles and protects me always."

- "I am abundant in the love of the Universe."

- "The strongest power in the Universe is love, and I hold that power within my soul."

Love Meditation

Take a few moments to clear your mind. Think of peaceful thoughts, do not resist any other thoughts that come into your mind, simply see them, and let them pass. Begin by taking in and releasing three deep and cleansing breaths. Imagine that you see yourself stepping from your door onto a beautiful fluffy cloud. Envision that this is a soft and comfortable cloud of perfect softness. As you drift onto the cloud notice the perfection of this day, it is beautiful, bright, clear, and at the perfect temperature. As you bask in this greatness, and goodness envision that you are lifted up high into the sky, safely and comfortably on this cloud. As you look around you see millions of sparks of light darting across the sky. Most are moving in the same direction forming an endless stream of light that is circling the Universe at the speed of light. Imagine that you see it creating a bright white circle around the Universe, and continues to travel around it again and again. With each circle the light becomes brighter and brighter. Imagine that your cloud is drawn closer to this energy of pure light. As you move closer, and closer you are able to feel the power in the light, this power gives you the feeling of over-whelming love. The closer you come to it, the stronger the feeling, and now you know you are in the presence of our Universal God source. Within this light there is no fear, no pain, no anger, and no sadness only complete and unconditional love. As you receive this love filling you completely you are also sending love out back to our Universal God source. You watch as your love joins perfectly with God's and begins to encircle the world.

The love and light from this union is so powerful your feelings are indescribable. Envision yourself remaining here for a while taking in this love, being recharged, with this love, being cleansed by this love, experiencing and sharing unconditional love. When you feel ready, allow yourself to slowly move away from the light, and as you do notice the intensity of the light dims. Notice that the soft cloud begins to slowly descend back to the earth, and as it does you remain connected with our Universal God source. Slowly the cloud makes its way back to earth, and you float effortlessly over rooftops, roads, fields, and back you are gently returned back to your home where you safely step off the cloud, and back into your home knowing that you are filled with the unconditional love of our Universal God source.

Remember
When you are challenged by the illusions of this world, you must not lose hope. Remember that you are forever connected to the direct source of unconditional love. Love is not an illusion, it is pure, it is true, and it is you. Look past all obstacles, and let the love of our Universal God guide you.

Journal Exercise for Love
Our Universal God is love, and love is what unifies us all as One. If you can accept the power of God's unconditional love as a

Universal truth, you can begin to awaken to the fact that you are eternally connected to that source, and It will answer your every desire in life. It's simple to achieve, just step over the threshold of doubt and fear, and open your mind.

Today we are going to make a list of loving thoughts, ideas, feelings, and attach them to an imaginary helium balloon, and release them unto the world to symbolize the spreading of our unconditional love to every living soul on the planet.

This is an exciting and creative exercise, and another opportunity for you to get in touch with you inner child. You get to imagine, and experience watching the joy and excitement of releasing a huge bundle of colorful balloons floating, and rising above the clouds. These balloons will take your messages of love to the Universe.

The most exciting and possibly challenging part of this exercise is that the notes you are going to attach to the balloons will include messages of all sorts. If there are individuals or situations you feel need love, you will write them a message. If there are individuals who you feel have wronged you or who you feel you have wronged, you are going to write them a message. If there are places in our country or in this world that appear to need more love because of what they are experiencing at this time, you can send them a message of love. Your messages of love can be sent and released to anyone, anything, and anywhere you choose. This is also an excellent opportunity to send messages of love to heal old wounds or to just send love to someone you are afraid to say "I love you" to in person. This truly is an exciting and fun exercise so do exactly that, have fun, enjoy it, and really project your love into it. Remember, the more excited you get, the higher your vibration, the higher the vibration, the more powerful, and the faster you will create the experience of receiving and sending love. That's the one thing we can all use more of!

Optional Exercise
Some people have chosen to literally create love messages, and have actually attached them to balloons and released them. Others have issues with the affects and damages this can have

to our environment. So you can create literal balloons by using colored construction paper. You can draw the shape of a balloon, and use a hole punch to make to tie colorful ribbon or string through the bottom. On the face of the balloon write your messages. Once you are finished creating your balloons you can decide to hang them from someplace significant without worrying about the effects to the environment or you can simply paste them on a wall in your home or special room. Your love messages can include messages as well as your personal desires to be released onto the Universe. You messages could read as follows:

- "I send love to my grandmother who is healing from surgery."

- "I send love to my daughter who is away at college and I miss her."

- "I send love to my husband who is away on business."

- "I send my love to my aunt who lives across the country."

- "I send love to the children in Africa who are struggling for food and water.

- "I send love to all women struggling with breast cancer."

- "I send love to individual suffering from mental health."

Desires
- "I release my desire for financial abundance to the Universe."

- "I release my desires to be pain free to the Universe."

- "I release my stress from my job to the Universe."

Conclusion

You can use this exercise to send love, appreciation, gratitude, and your desires. It is intended to symbolize your ability to release these things onto the Universe knowing that they will receive your love, appreciation or gratitude if that is what you desire.

In your journal write about this exercise, list the things you wrote on your love balloons. Record how this made you feel, and how it may have helped you get rid of some of the things you may have been carrying around with you. Also describe how this exercise helped you gain a closer relationship with our Universal God source.

TRANSFORMATION
MEDITATION

After completing this book you will have experienced a change, it is unavoidable. Something has been shifted in your life as a result of the information you have allowed to saturate your soul. As with every journey, there are experiences you have that cause an impact on your life no matter the depth of that experience.

There is an ancient Japanese proverb that says" An old man walked down the dirt road away from his home to the village and did not meet anyone along the road. He decided to walk back the other way toward home. Even though he encountered no one while on his journey, he was changed." So it is with you, as you travel down the road of life, no matter your encounters, you will always experience some form of change. Every chance meeting, deep thought, or book you read works to change your perspective in some manner. While this is a wonderful idea, think about how much greater the impact of this journey could be if you were to take the next step and actively move past the theory and began to actually incorporate the information from this book into your life, right now, TODAY. Can you imagine the transformation that could and would possibly take place?

If you haven't already received the experience of transformation, you are given one more opportunity to ignite the light that lies within you through this transformational meditation. This last meditation is designed to open your mind to the limitless possibilities to better your life which will ultimately lead to bring forth a more loving world for us all to enjoy.

Transformation Meditation

Utilizing the methods that have been outlined in the book, find a place and allow yourself enough time to move through all of the distraction that may occur. Allow yourself to hear the noises around you simply don't acknowledge or process what they are, or where they are coming from. Just let them be, hear them, and allow them to move on.

After you are relaxed, and you are sitting in a comfortable position, you may begin:

Envision yourself curled in a fetal position, enclosed in a tight cocoon which restricts your movement, but offers you safety, security, warmth, and love. Feel the serenity of peace, love, and goodness within this cocoon. While in this position, observe some aspects of your life that you would like to change. Think about goals you would like to achieve that would help make your life complete. Think on things you would like to accomplish after you are freed from this cocoon. In your mind, make a list of the reasons you believe you cannot achieve the goals you would set. Perhaps the reasons were that you believed that there was a lack of money in your life, or that you had a lack of education to acquire a particular job, whatever the reasons that you believe were obstacles to achieving the life you desire. As you list those reasons in your mind, notice how the cocoon tightens around you, restricting you even more; wrapping you tighter and tighter.

Now, envision in your mind the life you would truly desire if there were no restrictions or obstacles of doubt, or fear. It may be that you imagine yourself in a new home, or traveling with your family, or attending school, or with better health. Whatever it may be, see yourself living that life. Think about how that life would cause you to feel. Imagine the excitement, the happiness, contentment, enjoyment, sense of accomplishment. Stay there in those thoughts for as long as you can. Hold the images of you enjoying your life entirely; doing all those things you desire to do. As you imagine these joyous experiences, notice that the cocoon loosens with every happy thought. Imagine that the happier and more positive, and content you become the cocoon continues to loosen. If you come across an experience you are doubtful of, the cocoon tightens again. Allow yourself to have these wonderful thoughts of eternal happiness, and freedom, thoughts of an unlimited supply of all the things you choose.

As you become aware of how your thoughts of fear and doubt work to either keep you tightly snug within the cocoon, and how your thoughts of joy, happiness, and peace cause it to loosen. Make a conscious choice to choose the thoughts that better serve your higher self. Continue to envision your desires, and see yourself living that dream. As you continue those thoughts, feel yourself breaking free of the cocoon. Remember, each time feelings of doubt and fear creep in your freedom is canceled, and you remain concealed within the cocoon. Now, envision yourself free, soaring, gliding freely outside the cocoon, and watch as you are set free to soar. See yourself flying high above fear, and out of reach of doubt. Imagine that you have been transformed into a beautiful butterfly, soaring freely in the sky to experience what it is you choose. Stay there for awhile enjoying your life in flight, overcoming all your obstacles. See yourself flying freely, experiencing you life fully in flight!

It is our heartfelt desire that everyone experience enough of a change to be inspired to begin looking at how to transform your life, and create it to be the life you want to live. After completing this book you have gained new information, and may have had old information reaffirmed. You have completed this journey, and are now fully equipped to re create your life. The insight you've gathered along the way allows you to make your next steps with confidence. We suggest that you use your journal to reflect upon your new perspective, and to practice gaining the state of mind that will allow you to continue to elevate your vibration in order for you to attract and experience those things in life you desire.

As a final journal exercise please make an entry and record the following information and questions:

1. What are your desires, and or goals for your life?
2. What obstacles did you perceive kept you from experiencing your life as you desire?
3. What have you done with to overcome those obstacles?
4. What prayers have you used to help you achieve your desired goals?

As you achieve each one of your goals, make sure you record them in your journal so you can have on record your complete journey, and all that you were able to accomplish it upon completion of your journey.

CONCLUSION

Welcome, you have arrived, and have completed this Transformational Journey, and no doubt have experienced many different things that have impacted your life in many ways. It is time to celebrate, to explore, create, and find out who you have become, and to see yourself for who you really are after this spiritual metamorphosis. You will notice that some things have immediately changed, things you can feel, know, and can describe right now. There are also things that have begun to shift, and you may notice just a slight inclination of the shift. There are also things that have shifted ever so slightly but you are unable to notice and need more time and experience before it is completely manifest in your reality. All of these different variations of change are wonderful and awesome. They are all an indication of some kind of development which means that on each level you have allowed yourself to accept the information, and were able to find a place within yourself to store and nurture it. You were able to accept unconditional love from our Universal God source, and allowed it to saturate your soul, and there are very powerful benefits from that experience alone. So, congratulations again, you are on your way!

You may be having an experience of "understanding" after struggling to understand. It may feel as though a light bulb has been turned on, and now you "get it". That may be the feeling of your soul thanking you for allowing the acceptance of this information. It may be thanking you for finally allowing the connection. This may be what it feels like when your soul replies, "Yeeess!

You got it!" Thank you!" Know that there are still experiences that you simply may not have grasped yet, and that's okay. This simply means that you've found an area that you need to spend more time developing, and can do so by revisiting and continuing to use the building blocks of prayers, meditations, or journal exercises. Developing this life changing experience is like building a muscle, the more you use it, the stronger it becomes. So, if there is any part of this experience that you would like to strengthen, go back to it, construct, and reconstruct the blocks and build your way to a new experience. Keep using them and reconfiguring them until you receive that "understanding" or that rejoicing of your soul. Each time you use these building blocks you will create a new experience which will bring you closer and closer to the level of understanding and acceptance you are striving to achieve. A very important point to remember is that you should never feel stressed or as if you are trying to memorize study material. What you should keep in mind is that you are working to allow your mind to accept the concepts openly, and develop a level of understanding which enables you to create experiences you desire. These experiences are what help shape and affect your thoughts, feelings, and beliefs of the world around you. It is not necessary to completely understand and master these concepts in order to begin to create your life as you would have it. Having the awareness of them is enough to move you in the direction of gaining a deeper understanding. There is no hurry, there is no deadline, and you need only choose to have this knowledge in order to create the experiences you desire. This shouldn't be a process that causes you stress or discomfort. It is meant to enhance your life, not cause it burden. Your only real goals in life are to create experiences that you enjoy, and that will help you experience yourself as who you really are. The more experiences you create, the closer you become to **"Being"** who you really are.

With these thoughts in mind, let's go back and evaluate what experiences you did have, and determine how they impacted your ability to reach your higher good. Let's begin by taking a look at your journal, and journal exercises. Take some time to read your journal completely. Answer and record the following questions and information:

1. What was the overall theme of your journal experiences?
2. Were you motivated, were you skeptical, were you fearful or were you excited to learn more about yourself?
3. How easy was it for you to let go of your old thoughts, feelings, and beliefs?
4. Which ones were you not able to let go of?
5. How will they serve you, and how do they fit with your new beliefs and experiences?
6. How easy was it for you to accept change?
7. What experience did you have that most affected the feelings you had of yourself? Why?
8. What were your most important values when you began this journey?
9. How has that changed, if at all?
10. What experiences helped you the most in feeling more empowered? Why?
11. How has this feeling of empowerment affected your life.
12. Which prayer topics were you most interested in? Why?
13. Which journal exercise enabled you to make the most change? Why?
14. Which meditation impacted you the most? How were you impacted?
15. In what areas did you most notice you've changed?
16. How so and why?
17. How has your relationship with our Universal God source changed?
18. What was the single most important experience you had?
19. In what ways will you be able to apply what you now know in your life?
20. In what areas do you feel you gained the most strength? How so?
21. In what areas are you unclear? Why?

Now, go to your Personal Inventory Value Assessment (PIVA), and take a through look at it.

22. Is there more that you would like to add or change?
23. Have your values been affected by the experiences you have had?

If so, record those changes and add them to your PIVA. As your understanding develops and you gain and create more experiences, this PIVA will change as well. Remember, your thoughts, feelings, and beliefs affect your ideas and values. You may notice that things you would not have checked at the beginning as being important to you are now important. You may notice that things you thought or felt, have shifted, and now you think and feel differently. This is a wonderful sign; it means that you have allowed yourself to be affected by the Universe's unconditional love. Take your evaluation a bit further, and discover more of yourself:

EXTRA EXERCISE: NEW LETTER OF INTRODUCTION

Based on what you have discovered about yourself, write a letter in your journal as if you were introducing your (new) self to someone vey special, and important. Make sure in your letter you add the following information:

- What do you now like most about yourself?

- Describe yourself after your spiritual metamorphosis as if you were describing yourself to someone very special and important.

- What are your strengths?

- What are your greatest gifts?

- What makes this individual (you) so special and valuable?

- Describe how you've grown.

- Identify the assets this individual possesses.

- Describe the direction this individual's life will go in.

- Describe your appreciation of this person.

Compare the information you now have of who you really are, and the information of yourself before you completed this journey. Record how your thoughts about yourself have changed. Lastly, enter your statement or prayer of gratitude acknowledging all that you have learned, and now have to begin creating your life anew.

You have gained so much knowledge, even if you don't quite see it yet or are not able to acknowledge it yet. Your ideas and who you really are have shifted. You may not immediately recognize the changes. You may not be able to visualize your metamorphosis as that of a butterfly, your changes may appear minimal, and may occur every so slightly but none the less, you have made changes. That which your eyes cannot see, your soul knows, and is rejoicing. Allow yourself to rejoice as well, accept and declare your power. You are now conscious of who you are, you are now aware of your partnership with our Universal God source. You know that you are capable of making selective choices to manifest your experiences and desires. If you gained nothing more than that knowledge alone, you have increased your personal power tenfold! Your thoughts are greater, your feelings are greater, your beliefs are greater, combined your creative abilities are greater. This is who you now are... **GREATER!** You can declare that, **"I now know myself as being greater than who I was before!"** You can now move on to expect nothing less than greatness. The expectation of greatness is the runway or launch pad to a new beginning. It is time to prepare to experience your life in flight. It is now time for you to **soar!**

By the way, in case you weren't aware, that special and important person you were introducing "your new" self to, was YOU!

You are special, and you are important, than, now, and forever more.

One last reminder …

"The breeze of dawn has secrets to tell you. Don't go back to sleep. You must ask for what you really want. Don't go back to sleep. People are going back and forth, where the two worlds meet. The door is round and open. Don't go back to sleep."

~Jalal Uddin Rummi 1207-1273

FAMOUS QUOTES

"The greatest danger for most of us is not that our aim is too high, and we miss it, but that it is too low, and we reach it." ~ Michelangelo

"Out of clutter, find simplicity. From discord, find harmony. In the middle of difficulty lies opportunity." ~Albert Einstein

"Worry not that no one knows of you; seek to be worth knowing." ~ Confucius

"Let no one ever come to you without leaving better and happier. Be the living expression of God's kindness; kindness in your face, kindness in your eyes, kindness in your smile." ~ Mother Theresa

"I find that the harder I work the more luck I seem to have." ~ Thomas Jefferson

"Our deepest fear is not that we are inadequate. Our deepest fear is that we are powerful beyond measure. It is our light, not our darkness that most frightens us." ~Marianne Williamson

"Nothing great was ever achieved without enthusiasm." ~Ralph Waldo Emerson.

"Forgiveness is not a radial form of obedience it is a choice not in anticipation of receiving anything. It is an unselfish act of love." ~Unknown

"There is no end, for the soul there is never birth nor death. Nor having once been does it ever cease to be. It is unborn, eternal, ever existing, undying, and primeval…" ~The Bhagavad-Gita

"Let me recognize that my problems have already been solved." ~A Course in Miracles

"You are today where your thoughts have brought you. You will be tomorrow where your thoughts take you. ~ James Allen

"People who have great lives think and talk about what they love more than what they don't love. And people who are struggling, think and talk about what they don't love more than what they do love." ~ Rhonda Byrne b1951

"Nurture your mind with great thoughts, for you will never go any higher....than you think. ~Benjamin Disraeli 1804-1881

"You demonstrate love by giving it unconditionally to yourself. And as you do, you attract others into your life those who are able to love you without conditions." ~Paul Ferrini

"If you will assume your desire and live there as though it were true, no power on earth can stop it from becoming a fact." ~Neville Goodard

"The mind attracts the thing it dwells upon." ~Napoleon Hill

Become aware of what you are thinking and you will recognize a law between your mood and your surrounding circumstances.

Believe that you are what you want to be!

AFFIRMATIONS

I cannot be held back from what I truly desire for I attract my desires, and they come to me by way of the Universe.

My life is full of endless potential. That which I desire is well within my reach. I need only make the choice to experience if for it is to be manifested in my life.

I am a being of light, full of creative energy.

My thoughts, ideas, and beliefs attract my experiences; therefore I am careful and clear in what I think.

Abundance and prosperity are my destiny, and I am open to receive them.

Abundance flows through my existence with ease.

I transcend all apparent limitations.

I am capable of anything that I am truly committed to achieving.

I love and appreciate myself, and the power within me.

I honor the moment I live in right now. I do not fret about the yesterdays or the tomorrows.

GLOSSARY OF TERMS

Affirmations: A powerful and positive phrase stating what is so.

Aura: The luminous glow surrounding a figure or object.

Causation: The relation of cause and effect.

Conscious Mind: The Mind of God; as seen and reflected in all of creation.

Creative Mind: Commonly thought of as the feminine side in the balancing of the individual.

Desire: An individual's request to possess something.

Destiny: In line with the law of cause and effect, destiny is as a result of what an individual thinks.

Disease: The thought operates through the individual, but not belonging to the individual.

Ego: The conscious self or the inner person.

Energy: Always present and available; a state of possibilities.

Enthusiasm: A strong inspirational feeling beyond excitement.

Error: The outcome of an act because of ignorance causing one to fail to achieve what can be accomplished.

Failure: The omission of a desired function or performance, or falling short of a desired goal.

Faith: A mental attitude of trust, and belief in the invisible, something for which there is no proof.

Happiness: The balance of mind, body, and circumstances to bring about the state of inner peace and joy.

Healing: to make the entire person whole by understanding the unity of the mind and the body.

"I AM" declaration: The understanding and declaration of the God theory that unifies us with our Universal God source.

Illusion: Something that deceives or misleads us. The erroneous conclusions of man that often appear in the subjective Universe.

Inherited Tendencies: Those tendencies that are handed down from the core of our memory, i.e. race characteristics.

Karma: The mental tendencies of cause and effect. The idea that "You reap what you sow."

Law: There is only one Law which is without limit yet, we are limited in the understanding of the Law. The same law that can make us rich can make us poor, depending on how we understand and use the Law.

Love: Love is the purest emotion in the Universe. It's power exists through our Universal God source.

Manifestation: To bring forth, to make something evident. A demonstration of power with the materialization of idea and though put into mind.

Meditation: The method of reaching a heightened level of spiritual awareness; communication with our Universal God source.

Mental Image: To see with the mind's eye what we visualize, and do not yet possess in the physical world.

Metaphysics: The belief that God is Creative Intelligence. The study that goes beyond the law of physics.

Omnipresence: What is present, at all places, and at all times.

Omnipotent: The all powerful Universal God source.

Paradigm: A set of assumptions and values that constitutes a way of viewing for the community that shares them.

Positive Thought: Affirmative thought that moves one towards its objective.

Power: The energy that everything is and lives by.

Prosperity: The condition of thriving.

Quantum Physics: The science of physics that says that everything is connected everywhere at once.

Reality: the forms that man has molded by his thoughts. The truth about anything.

Self Realization: The realization that you are One with, and a part of our Universal God source.

Soul: The creative essence of human beings, reflecting back to what it is gathering from the Universe.

Theosophy: The teaching about God based on the Universal brotherhood of all humanity.

Unconscious: Unknown to, out of consciousness.

Universe: The entire universe is perfection. The one power that includes all that exists.

Universal God source: The creator of all things otherwise referred to as God

SOME UNIVERSAL LAWS

These are some of the immutable Universal Laws that we believe impact our lives. These are brief descriptions of these laws that you will see throughout the course of reading the book.

Attraction: Focused purpose will bring results. Thoughts, action as well as words produce negative and/or positive energies

Connection: We are all connected "Oneness"

Reciprocity: What you put out into the world, you get back.

Duality: For every negative there is a positive

Evolution: Change is constantly occurring

Responsibility: We are responsible for the choices we make. We have the power to change the conditions of our lives,

Synchronicity: There are meaningful coincidences for which there are no known causes.

Intention: Taking an action with the genuine desire to make a change

REFERENCES

Anderson, U. S. *Three Magic Words*, Los Angeles; Melvin Powers Wilshire Book Company 1954 Reprint

Clarke, Pat and Roebuck, Linda: *Seeds of Possibility: A Five Element Theory*, Spring Retreat; Maryland, Bon Secour Conference Center April 2011

Dyer, Wayne. W, *The Power of Intention- Learning to Co-Create Your World Your Way:* Carlsbad, Calif, Hay House, Inc. 2004 Reprint

Goswani, Kryananda, *Beginner's Guide to Meditation*, Chicago, The Temple of Kriya Yoga 1992 Reprint

Grabhorn, Lynn, *Excuse Me, Your Life is Waiting Playbook*, Charlottsville, VA Hampton Roads Publishing 2001

Hicks, Esther and Jerry, Ask and it is Given, Carlsbad, Californis, Hay House , Inc. 2004

Holmes, Ernest, *The Science of Mind a Philosophy, A Faith, A way of Life*, New York, Penquin Putnam Inc. 1998

Isabel Myers and Kathrine Briggs, *Myers-Briggs Type Indicator*, 1942

Kinnear,Willis , 30-Day Mental Diet, Marina del Rey California, DeVorss Press, 1963

Maloney, George, A., *Inward Stillness*, Dimension Books, New Jersey, 1975

Ponder, Catherine, *Open Your Mind to Prosperity*, Marina del Rey, California, DeVorss Press 1971

Taylor, Terry Lynn, *The Alchemy of Prayer: Rekindling Our Inner Life*, Tiburn, Calif , HJ Kramer Inc. 1996

Wolf, Fred Allen, *Mind into Matter: A New Alchemy of Science and Spirit*, Needham, MA Moment Point Press 2001.

Walsh, Neale Donald, Conversations With God - an uncommon dialogue, New York. G.P. Putnam's Sons 1995

Williamson, Marianne, *A Return to Love*, New York, Harper Collins 1992

Zukav, Gary, *The Seat of the Soul*, New York , Simon & Schuster, 1990

www.ingramcontent.com/pod-product-compliance
Lightning Source LLC
Chambersburg PA
CBHW060738050426
42449CB00008B/1259